RK NARAYAN

The Compassionate Chronicler of Indian Life

INDRADEEP BHATTACHARYYA

PAPER MISSILE
NIYOGI BOOKS

Published by
NIYOGI BOOKS
Block D, Building No. 77,
Okhla Industrial Area, Phase-I,
New Delhi-110 020, INDIA
Tel: 91-11-26816301, 26818960
Email: niyogibooks@gmail.com
Website: www.niyogibooksindia.com

Editor: Arkaprabha Biswas, Anwesha Panda
Layout: Shashi Bhushan Prasad
Cover design: Anurag Hira
Cover illustrator: Douluri Narayana

ISBN: 978-93-91125-56-1
Publication: 2023

Price: ₹299

Publisher's note: Every effort has been made to ensure the accuracy of the information presented in this book. The images used in this book come from either the public domain or from the public commons, unless otherwise stated. The publisher welcomes comments and feedback from readers, in order to improve future editions, at niyogibooks@gmail.com.

Printed at Niyogi Offset Pvt. Ltd., New Delhi, India

For Maa and Baba,

The first cause, uncaused

It is a poet's business only to ask questions; he cannot always expect an answer.

—RK Narayan

Narayan... wakes in me a spring of gratitude, for he has offered me a second home. Without him I could have never known what it is like to be Indian.

—Graham Greene

CONTENTS

INTRODUCTION

I sincerely hope that the venerable Bankim Chandra Chattopadhyay will forgive us if we are convinced by Meenakshi Mukherjee's persuasive argument that the Indian English novel was born only in the 1920s.[1] It is a fact universally acknowledged that Bankim wrote the first Indian English novel, *Rajmohan's Wife,* in 1864,[2] and his is a towering presence in the history of Indian prose fiction, vernacular or English.[3] However, Bankim did not exactly set the stage on fire when it came to the Indian English novel proper. Mukherjee finds only five noteworthy names from the five decades following the publication of *Rajmohan's Wife—Kamala, a Story of Hindu Life* by Krupabai Satthianandhan (1894), *The Prince of Destiny* by Sarath Kumar Ghosh (1909), *Hindupore, A Peep behind the Indian Unrest: An Anglo-Indian Romance* by SN Mitra (1909), *The Dive for Death: An Indian Romance* by T Ramakrishnan (1911) and *The Love of Kusuma: An Eastern Love Story* by Bal Krishna (1910). One can add Lal Behari Day's *Govinda Samanta, or The History of a Bengal Raivat* (1874) to this list. Throughout this half a century, the Indian novel in English maintained a semblance of life, but it did not have any genuine vitality. Ironically, the publication history of *Rajmohan's Wife* itself proves our point; it came out as a book only in the 1930s, over 60 years after it was written.

The troika of RK Narayan—Mulk Raj Anand—Raja Rao burst into the literary scene in the 1930s with the publication of *Swami and Friends* (1935), *Untouchable* (1935) and *Kanthapura* (1938) respectively. This was the decade when the 'Indian English novel' found a firm footing, and the importance of these three in ensuring that just cannot be overstated. Each of them was unique in his own way—Anand held up social problems in early 20th century India, Rao's domain was philosophy, Narayan focused solely on telling stories based on what he saw and knew (MK Naik calls Anand's style 'militant humanism', and finds in him a 'robust earthiness', as opposed to 'Narayan's delicate blend of gentle irony and sympathy, quiet realism and fantasy)'[4]—but perhaps, it would not be improper to say that Narayan's literary achievements far outshine those of the other two, at least in terms of the output. In a career spanning six decades, Narayan authored 15 novels, 7 collections of short stories (around 200 in total), 5 volumes of non-fiction, including memoirs, travelogues and personal essays and 3 books on mythology. He was the first global icon of Indian English literature, much before it became an institution and sent international markets into a tizzy.

Many years later, looking back at his achievements, Narayan was to describe his decision to pursue a career in writing fiction in English language in the 1930s as 'foolhardiness' to his biographers, Susan and N Ram. For a young graduate hailing from a middle-class Tamil family, it was a bizarre choice, to say the least. Moreover, before taking the leap of faith, he had just rejected going for an MA degree, and resigned from a school-teaching job after an altercation with the headmaster.

Headmasters, by the way, Narayan knew well. He was the second of RV Krishnaswami Iyer (RV stood for Rasipuram Venkatarama) and Gnanambal Iyer's eight children. Not long after Narayan's birth, Krishnaswami joined a school in Mysore as the headmaster, and the family shifted to the neighbouring state of Karnataka, leaving the infant in the care of his maternal grandmother in what was then known as Madras.

Narayan received his early education mostly at missionary schools, including the Lutheran Mission School and the Christian College High School. For the first few years of his life, he visited his parents only during vacations. Then the headmaster joined Maharaja's Collegiate High School and brought Narayan over to Mysore under his own care. It is in the library of this school that Narayan got initiated into serious literature. For the next several decades, Mysore would be his home.

In spite of that, throughout his life, Narayan was an Iyer from Madras at heart, and somewhat of an outsider amid Kannadigas. 'He is external to Kannadigas. That is how I see it,' says his lifelong friend, the noted sociologist MN Srinivas. Narayan's daughter Hema agreed to this, while talking to his biographers, 'recalling the subtle differences that distinguished her father from his five Mysore-raised brothers. For one thing, Narayan would never master Kannada the way his brothers did… his mother tongue was indisputably Tamil…'[5]

To go back to the issue of taking up writing fiction in English as his calling, it was something no one had heard of. His wife wondered how could writing stories be an alternative to a job! For the first few years of his life as a writer, all his submissions—from juvenile essays sent to Indian and British magazines to the manuscript of his first novel sent to all publishers across the country as well as many abroad—met with rejections.

At one point, his life almost mirrored a Sisyphean metaphor—sending a manuscript, waiting for about six weeks, receiving the manuscript back with a rejection note, and then sending it to another publisher, over and over again. It was valiant for him—and for Mulk Raj Anand and Raja Rao—to stick to this mission in the face of insurmountable obstacles. Anand's first noteworthy work, *Untouchable*, was rejected by 19 publishers over four years before finally making it to the press. They are the true heroes of what is now the global phenomenon, called Indo-Anglian or Indian English literature.

What primarily drove Narayan to making that choice was his craving for freedom, the taste of which he got in a rather unexpected way. Narayan had failed in his examinations, not once, but twice at the college level (unbelievably, once in English). The sudden reprieve from formal education gave him the opportunity to explore himself. These two years eventually became the turning point in his life. The fourth chapter, 'Becoming a Writer: A Leap of Faith', discusses it in some detail.

If one has to put a finger on what constitutes the essence of Narayan's writing across genres, one can't help but talk about compassion—a quality that permeates his writing so deeply that at times, questions have been raised whether his longer fictional works have enough critical realism to be called novels proper. Even the vilest of characters (they are very few in number) are treated with an affection and warmth that is typically Narayan-esque. It is this quality that distinguished him from his contemporaries and continues to give his writing its unmistakable flavour.

Compassion, the reader might agree, has great value in Indian moral life. According to *Brihadaranyaka Upanishad,* it was one of the *guna*s or cardinal virtues that the Prajapati asked his students to inculcate, at the end of their formal learning with him.[6] It is this particular quality of Narayan's worldview that made his fiction distinctly humane. Perhaps, that is why his writing felt like home, not only to millions of Indian readers, but also to Graham Greene, for whom Narayan's oeuvre defined Indianness.

The hallmark of Narayan's art lay in the feel of artlessness that it exuded. The story, rather than the technique of telling it, was of paramount interest to him. In a wonderful essay on Narayan's art, the Indian-born Canadian author Keith Garebian writes that Narayan's art reaches its pinnacle when he conceals his techniques—'recalling Dryden's familiar maxim that it is an art to conceal art.'[7]

If one has to identify one stylistic feature in his writing that is Narayan's signature, one cannot but talk about his humour. In subtlety, geniality and felicity, Narayan's humour is second to none in world literature. His fiction has abundant examples of this. He could inject humour into anything, even death. One instance that readily comes to mind is a passage where he talks about his father's death in his superbly written autobiography *My Days*. He writes: 'My father lived up to the last date of the month, as if to satisfy a technical need, and died, leaving us to draw his pension for the full month.'[8] John Thieme opens his brilliant monograph on Narayan by quoting the hilarious self-obituary Narayan wrote in the middle of his life. He imagines himself as being interrogated by the 'International Tribunal for Keeping an Eye on Novelists' and charged with offences such as writing too much and imagining a town with bad geography.

Other than the publishing industry and market forces, the other major concern for Narayan and his compatriots was of course the issue of language. Writing in pre-Independence India about India in the colonizer's language was fraught with risks of all kind. In 1938, Raja Rao described the problem in his iconic foreward to *Kanthapura* as follows: 'The telling has not been easy. One has to convey in a language, that is not one's own, the spirit that is one's own. One has to convey the various shades and omissions of a certain thought-movement that looks maltreated in an alien language. I use the word "alien", yet English is not really an alien language to us. It is the language of our intellectual makeup—like Sanskrit or Persian was before—but not of our emotional makeup.'[9] Narayan himself thought about it deeply in various stages of his life. In an essay titled 'To a Hindi Enthusiast', he writes, in his typical light-hearted vein,

> For me, at any rate, English is an absolutely *swadeshi* language. English, of course, in a remote horoscopic sense, is a native of

> England, but it enjoys, by virtue of its uncanny adaptability, citizenship in every country in the world. It has joined in India longer than you or I, and he is entitled to be treated with respect. It is my hope that English will soon be classified as a non-regional Indian language.[10]

This book is a monograph. It does not intend to offer a critical evaluation of Narayan's literary oeuvre, nor is it a detailed biography. A monograph, by definition, is somewhere in between. It is meant for any common reader who might have grown up watching *Malgudi Days* on television or browsing Narayan's books as pleasure reading or as school/college texts and ever since has wanted to dive deep into the author's life and times; or for someone who has always been amused by Swaminathan or Chandran, Raju, Savitri or any of the host of unforgettable characters Narayan created, and wants to know what went into the making of them. There might be others to whom Narayan's delightful weekly columns in *The Hindu* had brought unadulterated joy every Sunday morning for decades, and who knew him only from a distance, and are now keen to see how the author achieved his enormous breadth of vision. This monograph tells the behind-the-scenes story; it discusses the events, circumstances and people in Narayan's life who shaped him as a human being and author, and as far as his literary achievements are concerned, the monograph only aspires to present a bird's eye view of his corpus and an elemental discussion of his art.

As readers, we grow with every new book or author we read. And finally we come to love authors who are without any pretence. We may be in awe of those who are highly skilled and sophisticated in their art, but the innermost corner of a reader's heart is always reserved for authors who bare their soul and strip themselves of all affectations. To me, Rasipuram Krishnaswami Narayan Iyer was one such author. They don't make them like that anymore. In a world where it is more important to be clever than to be kind, to be ornate than to be honest, to be dashing than to be gentle, this book is a tribute to a true gentleman of an author who, in spite of all his fame, did not have a single pretentious bone in his body. May his legacy live on. May there be more RKNs.

1, VELLALA STREET

RK Narayan's earliest childhood memories were about a monkey and a peacock, two creatures that were the author's constant companions at his childhood home. At the age of two, Narayan was sent to his maternal grandmother's house situated at 1, Vellala Street, Purasawalkam, Madras, after his mother had given birth to a girl, the couple's fourth child. It is here that young Narayan was to spend the next 14 years of his life, under the supervision of his unforgettable grandmother.

If Malgudi is Narayan's Macondo,[1] Purasawalkam could well be Aracataca.[2] '...Puraswalkam, with its village traditions and small-town ambience, with its role of playing host to Narayan's formative years, could not escape making inputs into his fictional universe,' write Narayan's biographers Susan and N Ram.[3] In fact, the points of similarity between RK Narayan and Gabriel

Garcia Marquez do not end with the fact that both of them used fictional towns as their settings. They both were brought up by their maternal grandmother and both have recounted how uneasy they initially felt in the company of their mothers. And then, both of them started their career as journalists. But more about that later.

The house in Purasawalkam was a large, red-tiled bungalow with many rooms of different sizes, but most of them had been rented out, so that the family could make ends meet after the death of Tindivanam Narayanswami Iyer, the author's grandfather. In his autobiography *My Days*, Narayan recollects, 'Actually, our house was a big unit which my grandmother had partitioned and rented out to different offices and stores and families, keeping only a kitchen, living room and my uncle's upstairs room, for our own use. I did not realize at that time how much she depended on the rents for our survival.'[4] The house was situated on a corner plot at the intersection of Vellala Street and Puraswalkam High Road, and young Narayan spent hours sitting at the veranda, observing the slow but steady flow of life.

The sights, smells and sounds of his early life in Madras stayed with Narayan forever. As the young boy sat at the door with the peacock, passers-by would stop to admire the beauty of the pet. For reasons diverse, people of many quarters of the society used to come to meet his grandmother—mendicants, vegetable-sellers, the tailor, the goldsmith and many more. The author's niece Janaki, who lived in the same house a few years after Narayan, later recounted that the door of the house was open for everyone at all hours. In those days, however, the peacock often chased away strangers if they stepped in without a warning. Sitting at the door, Narayan learnt, among other things, the first swear words coming from a shop-owner across the street as he cursed his habitual debtors. Then his words would be drowned in the noise of the tram entering the terminus a stone's throw away and screeching to a halt.

Most of the time, however, Narayan was out on the streets, exploring the lanes and by-lanes with a gang of friends, rolling his iron hoop, *dhoti*s brought up to his knees. Vellala Street, Audiappa Mudali Street, Gangadeswarar Road and Purasawalakam High Road formed a large rectangular perimeter that they traversed barefoot multiple times every day under the scorching Madras sun. It was a carefree time with no one to admonish them. A few in the group did not have the hoops or bicycle rims; they simply ran with others imagining they had something in their hands. At the end of the day, when the streetlights came on, the boys dispersed, certain to meet the following morning.

Apart from the pets, the other companion Narayan had in his early childhood was his maternal uncle, TN Seshachalam, the elder of his mother's two brothers. Narayan fondly remembers the time spent in his company in the initial pages of *My Days*. To his biographers Narayan said, 'Grandmother, Seshachalam and mother were of one type—principled.'[5] Seshachalam was a college-goer in Narayan's childhood; more importantly, he was a talented photographer who had a tripod and his own dark room for developing pictures. One of Narayan's earliest photographs is by Seshachalam, and it is indeed a magnificent one in which the author's large and deep eyes would stand out to any viewer. Apart from photography, Seshachalam took keen interest in literature. Though he was training to become a lawyer, he pursued literature throughout his life with dogged resilience. For seven years, despite dwindling finances, he almost single-handedly brought out a Tamil literary magazine called *Kala Nilayam*. There is little doubt that the haunting character of Srinivas in *Mr Sampath—The Printer of Malgudi* was largely based on Seshachalam.

Narayan's recollection of life at 1, Vellala Street, makes it clear that at a very tender age, he learnt to find unbridled joy in the simplest things of life, which would, in later years, lend an infectiously cheerful quality to his fiction. He narrates, with meticulous details, the evening when his uncle took him shopping for the first time. The streets lined with colourful shops seemed like a wonderland. The first thing that fascinated him was an old man in khaki coat and blue turban, who carried a ladder on his shoulder and went about lighting up the street lamps. The unhurried, measured efficiency of the man captivated the boy's mind. Clinging on to his uncle's fingers, he watched him in awe as the man set up his ladder against a pole, climbed it up, opened the lid of the hexagonal glass lamp, cleaned it with a cloth, filled it with oil, lit up the wick, closed the lid, climbed down, balanced the ladder on his shoulder and moved to the next pole.

The boy wanted to ask him his name, where he came from, what he did with the ladder when he slept and many such inescapable questions, but they remained forever unanswered, as his uncle, with his adult disregard for the lamplighter's wonder world, walked away briskly.

Walking further ahead, a sweet shop, run by a bespectacled man with a shining gold chain around his neck, caught the boy's eyes. Sitting at his doorstep, he had always felt hungry at the delectable smell of fried delicacies coming from some nearby yet unknown source. That day, his uncle decided to buy some mouth-watering stuff for him, wrapped in brown palm-leaf. The young boy wasted no time in gorging on the delicacies even as he struggled hard to save himself from speeding cyclists, marauding cows and rampaging milkmen with large cans. The only dampening sight in an otherwise dream sequence was that of an orange school building with a green gate, where the uncle promised young Narayan would soon find himself in. His first and final impression of the Lutheran Mission School was that of repulsion.

An unusual character he remembered from his early days was Kodandam, the muscular, *lathi*-wielding fuel merchant, whose shop opposite Narayan's house played an important part in the annual festival of local deity Ponni Amman ('rice goddess'). Once every year, the deity was taken out of the sanctum sanctorum and carried in a colourful procession to the fuel shop and placed on a decorated pedestal for 10 days and the whole of Vellala

Street would wear a festive look. Apart from the rituals, what intrigued Narayan more was the host—he would stand guard with his *lathi* in front of the goddess for the whole period, occasionally putting his skills with the bamboo pole on display. The young boy would sit on the window-sill to enjoy the festive atmosphere.

One evening, however, he saw Kodandam moving about in their garden. He was scared out of his wits under the fixed belief that the man was there to teach him a lesson, though for what offence he did not know. He ran for cover and hid himself under a pile of clothes to be sent for wash. The entire household, including the tenants, started looking for him, but the young boy kept sitting there in darkness for hours, partly in fear of the roving *lathiyal* and partly basking in the pride of finding an infallible hiding place. Eventually, the police had to be informed of the missing boy. However, before they pressed themselves into action, the pressing need of hunger put an end to the child's persistence and he emerged out of nowhere announcing that he was hungry. It was perhaps this incident that made it abundantly clear to everyone that it was high time the boy was sent to school.

Little Narayan had large eyes and curly hair falling down to his cheeks; but more than these, his self-proclaimed resemblance with Rama, the family's pet monkey, made him immensely proud. When he boasted of this to his grandmother, she was understandably scandalized. 'What a fool to want to look like a monkey! You are in bad company,' she said.[6] As in those childhood years, as throughout his celebrated life, even at the height of fame, Narayan always remembered not to take himself too seriously. This attitude of geniality and self-effacement eventually became the source of the impeccably subtle humour in his writing.

Parvathi, Narayan's maternal grandmother, was known to the entire locality as 'Ammani'. In interview after interview in his later life, the author would credit her with being the most important person in his early life and describe her as an extraordinary woman deserving a book devoted completely to her. In his autobiography *My Days* and his last published book, the semi-fictional *Grandmother's Tale*, Narayan delightfully recollects the time spent with Ammani in the most impressionable years of his life. She was a storyteller par excellence, a trait Narayan picked up from her, and an expert gardener who spent much of her time amid her large family of plants which included many species of hibiscus, roses, innumerable exotic flowers, various kinds of jasmine, et cetera. When a plant died, she often shed tears and cursed the tropical weather of Madras.

When Narayan returned from school, she would make it a point to examine what he had been taught. On most occasions, she would be unsatisfied. And at those moments, she took it upon herself to make up for the inefficiency of the teachers at school. She would interrupt her gardening to sit with the boy in an easy chair and teach him many a lesson—multiplications, the Tamil alphabet and sayings by ancient Tamil scholars. She would also make him memorize Sanskrit verses in praise of Saraswati. Some days, she would hum a few tunes and the young pupil was tasked with identifying the *ragas*. She was methodical and firm. Ammani would serve dinner to the boy only after he satisfactorily completed his lessons. To prevent the boy from dozing off, she would keep a bowl of water handy, patting his eyes with her moist fingers from time to time. She also maintained a diary, keeping note of the child's academic progress. She was a loving grandmother with the air of a school inspector, an adult Narayan later felt.

Narayan's grandmother was the go-to person for the villagers for all sorts of reasons. She went out of her way to help people. Matchmaking, in particular, was one of her skills much in demand. She could read horoscopes and used her influence to seal marriage deals. People often came to her for discussion on other matters of vital importance. She carried on the discussions while tending to her family of plants in the garden. She knew their medicinal values as well. If someone came writhing in pain from a scorpion bite (it was quite a common affair in the village), she would apply a paste made of crushed leaves and make the afflicted person chew a few leaves, with an air of assurance about the validity of the medication and would often go to an extent of crediting the *Ramayana* as its source. She had an exercise book where she noted down the cure for various common diseases.

A young Narayan observed her in awe as Ammani became busy with myriad preparations before taking him to his parents in Chennapatna in Mysore during his summer holidays. She would be particularly concerned with making various kinds of delicacies, some of which would be in preparation for months in advance. Overall, it was like a ceremony. At her son's slightest objection, Ammani would give the unassailable excuse that Gnana, her elder daughter, was sick and weak and she just couldn't visit her grandchildren empty-handed.

The raw materials came from a cooperative shop which functioned from one part of the house. Returning from school, Narayan would be delighted to see numerous packages and gunny bags full of groceries strewn on the floor. There would be a battalion of helpers working at Ammani's instructions, 'pounding and sifting and grinding and mixing and kneading…'[7] The house buzzed with activities. Delicacies of different shapes, sizes and tastes would be spread over mats under the sun to be dried. Narayan and other younger members of the family were then given the critical task of keeping birds and insects away. Waving and screaming at crows to scare them away at times earned him an anna at the end of the day. The occasional indiscretion of quietly slipping into some half-dried treats into his mouth from the mats was, of course, the other secret reward.

At the end of it all, numerous containers would be ready to be dispatched to various relatives, but Narayan's mother's share would certainly be the largest. Reading the description of these episodes in *My Days*, one can't help admiring Narayan's keen observation skills even at that tender age. Not only did he notice every single detail, but he also remembered them decades later while writing his memoirs. Life, after all, 'is not what one lived, but what one remembers and how one remembers it in order to recount it.'[8]

Parvathi was a wise, big-hearted, benevolent and disciplined woman. What Narayan learnt from her is not easy to sum up in a few lines. One can say he learnt from her all that is worth learning, but most importantly, the gaze with which to observe life—a vision, a particular perspective of life, marked by moderation and generosity.

SCHOOL DAYS IN MADRAS AND MYSORE

Whoever has read the first few pages of Narayan's debut novel *Swami and Friends* already knows quite a lot about the author's school days, because he used almost every detail of his own early experiences in school and applied it to Swaminathan.

Narayan began his schooling at the age of six when he was admitted to ELM Fabricius Lutheran Mission School, more commonly known as just ELM to every student, a few blocks away from his home in Puraswalkam. It was the beginning of a real struggle, one might say. He was to go to three different schools during his stay in Madras—CRC High School and Madras Christian College High School being the other two—but he felt more or less the same everywhere: like a fish out of water. In 1922, Narayan's father decided to have him brought over to Mysore under his watch and he completed his school education at

Maharaja's Collegiate High School, where his father was the headmaster.

Rancour or extreme bitterness are words that one doesn't really associate with Narayan's worldview or writings, yet it is exactly these sentiments that are reflected in his recollection of his early days in school. His first impression of the ELM building with the crucifix at the top was disgust. The first day was miserable indeed, as the boy wept in nervousness and sat at the back. One of the first tasks he was given in kindergarten class was to shape a mound of clay into various fruits—a task in which he failed spectacularly. Then there was the ubiquitous cane, in almost every teacher's hand, that added to his woes. With time, the young boy came to identify the headmaster with only his cane—six whacks on the palm with the option of taking all of those in one or dividing those into three per palm being his most trusted mode of instilling discipline among students.

The other aspect of school life that he found deeply problematic was the examination system. Anxiety, sleeplessness, desperate nervousness, grimness are some of the words he uses in his autobiography to describe the annual April ordeal of tests and their effect on him. The climax of this antipathy was to come a few years later when he actually flunked the university entrance examination (and most shockingly, he failed in English).

The most dreadful experience for Narayan at ELM, however, had got to do with religious discrimination. In his autobiography, Narayan plainly states that the Christian teachers and students displayed a lot of hatred towards the non-Christians; Hindu gods and goddesses were lampooned and idolatry was derided as inferior to the cult of Jesus Christ. As the only Brahmin boy in the class, Narayan was often the target of the anti-Hindu invective.

Many such incidents come alive in *Swami and Friends*. For example, the day Mr Ebenezar, the scripture master, went fanatic:

> 'Oh, wretched idiots!' the teacher said, clenching his fists, 'Why do you worship dirty, lifeless, wooden idols and stone images? Can they talk? No. Can they see? No. Can they bless you? No. Can they take you to Heaven? No. Why? Because they have no life. What did your Gods do when Mohammed of Gazni

> smashed them to pieces, trod upon them, and constructed out of them steps for his lavatory? If those idols and images had life, why did they not parry Mohammed's onslaughts?'
>
> He then turned to Christianity. 'Now see our Lord Jesus. He could cure the sick, relieve the poor, and take us to Heaven. He was a real God. Trust him and he will take you to Heaven; the kingdom of Heaven is within us.' Tears rolled down Ebenezar's cheeks when he pictured Jesus before him. Next moment his face became purple with rage as he thought of Sri Krishna: 'Did our Jesus go gadding about with dancing girls like your Krishna? Did our Jesus go about stealing butter like that arch-scoundrel Krishna? Did our Jesus practice dark tricks on those around him?'
>
> He paused for breath. The teacher was intolerable to-day. Swaminathan's blood boiled. He got up and asked, 'If he did not, why was he crucified?'[1]

The Biblical stories, however, enchanted the young boy. The Old Testament seemed full of fascinating characters and he often identified with them. Guruswami, who taught them English, Tamil and mathematics, lived in the school building itself and often sent Narayan on errands like buying *paan* or tiffin for him. Narayan considered him a friend. There was also Mtityunjayam, who taught history and geography, a mild-mannered man. Narayan's fond recollection of them in his memoirs shows he did not hate his teachers as much as he hated the education system followed in missionary schools.

After studying at ELM for nine years, Narayan was admitted to CRC High School for what was then called the 'fourth form'. It didn't necessarily alter anything except the fact that this school was a bit farther from his home, and he had to pass through the shopping area to reach the school beyond the tram terminus. His brief stay at CRC was significant not for anything academic but for facilitating his first brush with some kind of political awareness. Around this time, Narayan got enthusiastic about joining the Scouts, but not after the ideal of Baden-Powell, the British founder of the worldwide movement, but following Annie Besant, who was a noted nationalist leader and the champion of the idea of Home Rule. The three-finger salute that Baden-Powell devised originally stood for service to God, Crown and Country; but in Narayan's case, it came to stand for God, Freedom and India. When they sang the anthem in the tune of 'God Save the King', what they actually felt was 'God save our Motherland!' Scout activities involved doing at least one good deed every day, like helping a visually impaired person cross the street or applying first-aid to an injured man, and Narayan tried his best to spot a man on the streets who needed some assistance with something.

Though cricket was Narayan's lifelong passion, at CRC he took a lot of interest in football, and was part of a team called Jumping Stars.

After spending a year at CRC, Narayan managed to get admission in the prestigious Christian College High School, thanks to his uncle Seshachalam's connections. The school, very close to the sea beach, was housed in a magnificent building in George Town, more than four miles from Puraswalkam. Commuting to and from significantly broadened Narayan's horizon as he had to pass through the heart of the city by a tramcar. He felt proud of his new school. The gentle and well-dressed teachers, students, the stately building with a Gothic tower, the spacious corridors, the chapel, large classrooms and a well-stocked library—all contributed to make Narayan, for the first time, happy being in school.

It was, however, a short-lived glory. In 1922, on his father's instructions, Narayan shifted to Mysore and joined his father's school. Both Dr Anderson, the headmaster of Christian College and Seshachalam wrote to his father pleading him to let the boy continue at the Madras school, reminding him that getting a seat there was itself a matter of prestige. His father, however, would have none of it.

***

The relocation to Mysore changed many things in Narayan's life. In his memoirs, Narayan calls it the end of 'one phase in my life' and the beginning of another as a Mysorean henceforth. With its architecture bearing evidence of its rich royal past and its hilly terrain, Mysore's cityscape was distinctly different from Madras. Though the era of the *Maharaja*s was long gone, a princely culture was still central to the city's life and ethos. Also, whereas the heat of Madras was often unbearable and young boys often roamed bare-bodied, in the cool climate of Mysore, one had to dress properly with a coat and cap; but above everything else, what mattered the most is the fact that the relocation brought him close to his family—his parents and siblings: Pattabhi (born in 1903), Janaki (1905), Alamelu (1909), Srinivasan (1911), Balaraman (1917), Ramachandran (1919) and Laxman (1922).

Weaver's Lines, the locality where the Narayans dwelt at that time, was in the suburbs. The family lived in a bungalow with high compound walls and a garden in front. A few years later, they shifted to 1087, Bojjanna Lines, which was a single-storey house with a red-tiled roof. Narayan and his elder brother Pattabhi lived in a room detached from the main building. In the late 1920s, after Krishnaswami had retired from service, the Narayans moved to another suburban neighbourhood called Laxmipuram, which was home to upper-middle-class families. Narayan lived there till 1967. Then he moved to Yadavgiri, where he had built his own house. Life in a southern Indian suburb, its bungalows, streets and extensions feature prominently in all of Narayan's fictional writings.

The constant company of his parents was something totally new to the teenager. Narayan's father and mother were studies in contrast. Krishnaswami was the proverbial headmaster—reticent, solemn and a strict disciplinarian. Gnanambal, on the other hand, was affectionate and easy-going. They both were, however, righteous and liberal-minded in their lifestyles. Krishnaswami was born in Salem in Tamil Nadu district and had migrated to Madras after finishing school. Gnanambal was his second wife. At home, as in school, he liked discipline, punctuality and orderliness.

During his Madras days, on one of the vacations when he had gone to live with his parents in Chennapatna, Narayan had witnessed with horror Krishnaswami slapping one of his sons over a dispute with a cycle shop owner. Since that day, he was afraid of his father and decided to avoid his presence. In his autobiography, Narayan paints a vivid and awe-inspiring picture of his father:

> As a person, he had a commanding personality, a senatorial voice, a sharp nose and a lion-like posture. A man who didn't fuss about children openly and never sat around and chatted... He moved in fixed orbits at home. He had a well-worn route from his room to the dining or bathroom, set hours during which he could be

> seen at different points and if one kept out of his way, as I thought then, one was safe for the rest of the day.[2]

In his first novel, *Swami and Friends*, the character of Swami's father, who is a lawyer by profession, is almost an exact replica of Krishnaswami. Swami's behaviour in his father's presence is in many ways identical to Narayan's in a similar situation. Tension mounted whenever their paths crossed—like in the novel when Swaminathan makes a list of stationery articles he needs before the exam, and his father rejects the whole idea at once. In at least two short stories, 'Father's Help' and 'A Hero', Narayan explored the nature of father-son relationships. In his second novel, *The Bachelor of Arts*, Chandran's father is an important character, and once again the relationship between the ageing father and the college-going son is based on adult Narayan's dealings with his father.

Krishnaswami was almost always impeccably dressed in a tie and a white turban. After school, he spent time in clubs and played tennis with his friends. The moment he returned home at night, the atmosphere would change abruptly. All the shouting and playing and running around would cease. At dinner, his father's presence meant the mischief-mongering was limited to giggles and glances exchanged. Only when it was ascertained beyond any doubt that Krishnaswami had retired to his bedroom for the day, the boys went back to being boys, throwing pillows and blankets at each other.

It was usual for fathers in those days to maintain an emotional distance with sons. So Krishnaswami didn't interfere much in his sons' lives. Narayan notes that his father communicated very little with him or his brothers, though he was quite at ease in the company of his daughters. The activities that relaxed him were playing the veena and spending long hours reading in his well-stocked library. It is only natural that his literary and artistic interests percolated into his sons. At home, he not only saw to it that the children converse in English but also made sure that they speak the language correctly and idiomatically. After his death, Narayan had found an English short story by his father in his school magazine.

Quite contrary to what would be expected from such a man, Krishnaswami had no faith in the examination system. 'He never bothered about examination results. He always displayed sympathy for a fallen candidate…'[3]

When Narayan failed his university entrance test, his father did seem concerned, not because the boy had failed as such, but because he had failed in English of all subjects; proficiency in which was a matter of social prestige. Narayan takes great comfort in saying in his autobiography that one very pleasant quality that his father had was his lack of faith in school examinations.

And it ran in the family. Years later when Hema, the author's daughter, refused to study arithmetic because she did not find it interesting, Narayan never demurred. Even when his grandson showed the slightest aversion to school, Narayan threw his full weight behind the youngster. In *My Days*, Narayan says his views on school education only got bolstered by reading Tagore, who himself famously rejected school curriculum, and was for much of his childhood, taught at home by private masters. 'I was opposed to the system of being prescribed a set of books by an anonymous soulless body of textbook prescribers, and of being stamped good or bad as a result of such studies,' writes Narayan.[4]

Narayan doesn't talk much his mother in his autobiography, *My Days.* In his other autobiographical work, *My Dateless Diary*, there are glimpses of the homemaker Gnanambal. Narayan's daughter Hema recollected to the author's biographers that her grandmother was a beautiful woman who looked resplendent in a saree and was a very methodical person. She was a voracious reader in Tamil and had even read Shakespeare in translation.[5] Besides, she was also an expert in applique work and various indoor games like chess and cards. One of her playmates was none other than the queen of Mysore.

There would be occasions when she went to the royal palace for a game and for dinner. The youngest brother, legendary cartoonist RK Laxman recollected to Susan and N Ram that Gnanambal's occasional absence from home caused anxiety not only in the children but also in her husband. And then she would come back—at times in a Rolls Royce—much to everybody's delight and awe. Many years later, Hema further recollected that when Gnanambal narrated her experiences at the palace to her family members, she would display a fine sense of humour and a wonderful style of storytelling. At times, such post-dinner chats would continue for hours, sometimes till midnight.

While Krishnaswami was, according to Narayan, neither religious, nor irreligious, Gnanambal was quite a devout lady. She had a strong sense of morality and her daily routine included fixed timings for prayers. At the same time, she was a tolerant woman. 'When Lakshman, refusing to be tired to any formal religion, removed and threw away after its ceremonial investiture the sacred thread worn by all orthodox male Brahmins, his mother's reaction was to laugh and praise his original thinking.'[6]

There are glimpses of Gnanambal in the mothers in Narayan's early fiction—the confident mother of Swaminathan in *Swami and Friends* who could have her way against her husband, the devout mother of Chandran in *The Bachelor of Arts* or the expert homemaker and mother of Krishna, Narayan's own reflection, in *The English Teacher*.

MAKING OF THE AUTHOR'S MIND

While paying his tributes to TS Eliot, noted literary critic William Empson had famously said, 'I do not know for certain how much of my own mind he (Eliot) invented…' By all means, it was an extraordinary observation—to attribute the creation of one's mind to another person. What creates/shapes a writer's mind and sensibilities? Most certainly, the quality and quantity of his early readings. Narayan was extremely fortunate in this context.

While living in Madras, Narayan had heard his uncle talk about Shakespeare. Seshachalam, then a college student, was a member of a drama club. Returning home in the evening, he would often narrate to his young nephew how they were planning to recreate the various scenes of *The Tempest*, or how a fellow actor was portraying a particular character. Long before Narayan read any serious literature, he knew Prospero and Caliban, and a few more things about Shakespearean romance.

Narayan's first brush with serious literature took place in his school library in Mysore, where he enjoyed a special access, being the headmaster's son. RV Krishnaswamy Iyer was the headmaster of Maharaja's Collegiate High School (established in 1833 as Raja's Free School and now known as Maharaja High School & Pre-University College) in Mysore from 1921 to 1927. Coming to live in Mysore from Madras, Narayan missed the busy life of the big city, and his former school, the Madras Christian Collegiate High School, being a part of which was glorious in itself.

As the young boy started acclimatizing to the new setting, he realised that studying in his 'father's' school had its own rewards. The most enjoyable and certainly the most significant among them was his easy access to the library. During the summer vacations, the librarian would throw open the bookshelves to the little boy, which he believed could keep him in good books of the headmaster. Young Narayan, already a voracious reader, made the best use of the opportunity, and a world of dreams opened up to him, a world that he was to inhabit for the rest of his life.

During holidays, Narayan would read all the magazines laid out on the tables and then take out books from the large shelves—four at a time—and read them at a stretch. One of the first books he read and remembered throughout his life was Sir Walter Scott's *The Bride of Lammermoor*. This and six other novels by Scott that he had read at that time created in the young boy a taste for literary romance. The tales set in the misty Scottish Highlands with 'strong-willed men and forlorn women in their castle homes'[1] captivated the mind of the young boy. And then there was no looking back. Next, he devoured Dickens. Then came Marlowe. And Moliere. And Tolstoy. And Thomas Hardy. Not one title, but many by each of the writers. Romances by Marie Corelli and the adventure fiction of Rider Haggard too made it to Narayan's desk. He read whatever he could lay his hands on.

The other person to benefit from his father's school library was Narayan's elder brother, Pattabhi, the eldest of the eight siblings. The two young boys would compete with each other on finishing off titles as fast they could. The elder brother would often guide the younger one to interesting books or read out passages from Shakespeare or Moliere. They would take a break only for meals. Days would pass without them realising. They had a world of their own, as Narayan recollects much later.

It might seem unusual for a school boy, but in addition to fiction, Narayan enjoyed reading history of English literature. William J Long's *English Literature* was one of the books that held Narayan in rapt attention. The edition that he read had a facsimile of the Magna Carta on its cover. One could say this is where young Rasipuram stood out from the boys of his age. These were early signs that he would excel in his pursuit of literature in his future years. At the tender age of 16 or 17, he tried to read the Old English epic *Beowulf*, though he found it baffling. Edmund Spenser too was disconcerting. But he enjoyed reading about the history of English literature Jacobean age onwards. Eventually, he made it a point to devote an hour every day to a systematic study of the same. It did not excite him as much as fiction did, but as was his wont, he stuck to it with a missionary zeal. He simply loved reading about the life and times of past authors.

Of all the fiction he read, he loved tragic novels the most. The Victorian novel *East Lynne* by Henry Wood moved him to tears. The other novel he absolutely loved was HG Wells' *Passionate Friends*. Corelli, however, was surely his favourite. Later in his adult life, he tried to reread some of these books, but found them quite uninteresting. 'In a state of juvenile innocence, the mind absorbs the essence through all the dross,' he observes in his autobiography.[3]

Narayan's high school reading room was the place where the seeds of his future success as a writer were sown. The headmaster saw to it that the library was well stocked. Young Narayan would eagerly look forward to the weekends when the foreign mail arrived with international magazines, wrapped in brown paper. They included *Little Folks* (published from Boston), *The Boys' Own Paper* (a British literary magazine), *Nineteenth Century and After* (British monthly that was a staple for intellectuals across the world), *Strand Magazine* (famous for publishing Sherlock Holmes stories for the first time in the UK; it printed 38 of them in total) and *Cornhill* (William Makepeace Thackeray was its founding editor). The magazines would be on the headmaster's desk by Sundays and had to be put on the shelves on Monday morning; so Narayan had to make the best use of the Sunday afternoons and evenings. Narayan was introduced to many English authors, including Sir Arthur Conan Doyle and PG Wodehouse, through these journals.

The Bookman (published in New York) offered Narayan a peep into the lives of authors and poets like Shelley, Keats and Hardy. He read in them details about their writerly lives, including how much they earned in royalty and what they thought of each other. Sitting in Mysore, he could visualize the throbbing literary world of London; its myriad characters came alive in front of his eyes. *The Atlantic* (founded among others by Ralph Waldo Emerson), *Harper's* (which is still in circulation and was the embryonic form of HarperCollins Publication), *Manchester Guardian* and *The Times Literary Supplement* gave him access to serious literature and literary criticism while weeklies like *John O' London Weekly* offered literary gossip and anecdotes.

Apart from acquainting young Narayan to the best of world literature, the other major thing that these magazines taught him was the art of selection and rejection. A single day was, of course, inadequate for reading all these; so Narayan gradually learnt to pick and choose. It developed in him a critical faculty. He no longer just read, but appreciated and reflected too.

Libraries, incidentally, went on to become one of Narayan's lifelong fascinations. In a wonderfully humorous essay titled 'A Library Without Books',

Narayan lamented (yes, he could do that—lament with the finest humour) our misplaced priorities as far as library policies were concerned. The biggest impediment for libraries, he writes, is the fact that governments have begun to take interest in them. He tells the story of a newly set up library where he saw every single detail being taken care of with utmost sincerity.

The fact that so much attention was being paid to the preparations for the inauguration ceremony of a library in a small town gave the author immense satisfaction. Even the names of the technicians, plumbers, electricians and sanitation workers were written in golden letters on big boards at the site.

Basking in that joy, he sought out one of the men behind the initiative, and asked him about the procurement of books. The man said they hadn't thought about books yet; all they were concerned with was the inauguration ceremony. A bit taken aback, Narayan prodded further about the plans for buying books. A brief conversation revealed that it was the last thing, if at all, in the founders' mind. Narayan concludes the essay with a summary of what he had gathered about the library. He writes:

> Building Rs 2,00,000; lighting Rs 15,000; plumbing etc Rs 12,000; garden layout and supervisors' charges Rs 5,000; counters shelves and furniture Rs 30,000; opening ceremony: printing of invitations, welcome address, president's speech and secretary's report Rs 2,000; pandal and tea Rs 4,000, and books: no budget yet.[4]

After finishing school, Narayan's failure in the university entrance examination in 1925 gave him a lot of time to read as he pleased, as he had an entire year at his disposal. He enjoyed this time in the company of nature and books. He spent the idle mornings sitting under a tree beside the Kukanahalli Lake, reading Palgrave's *Golden Treasury* or Rabindranath Tagore's *Gitanjali* or the poetry of Shelley, Keats, Byron and Browning. Cattle grazed in the distant fields, birds of various kinds gathered around the brimming water and Narayan immersed himself in his books. Sometimes he would go back to the lakeside in the afternoon to enjoy the sunset. Nature revealed herself to this young boy in her full glory. Tagore's poetry swept him off his feet.

The Scottish essayist and Victorian ideologue Thomas Carlyle was one author Narayan did not enjoy at all, but was forced to read since he was his father's personal favourite. Thomas Babington Macaulay and James Anthony Froude too belonged to this category. The headmaster regularly read these authors late into the night and felt strongly that his son should follow suit. The son had no choice. By his own admission, Narayan found them terrifying and 'unreadable',[5] but read the essays anyway to prove himself worthy. While he struggled with Carlyle or Macaulay, he couldn't but marvel at his father's penchant for such austere, deadpan writing.

Writing in July 1987, in the introduction to his collection of essays titled *A Writer's Nightmare*, Narayan pointed out that as far as he could remember, he was first drawn to personal essays where one could get a glimpse of the author himself, the kind perfected by Charles Lamb and Robert Lynd, among others. He loved the form because it 'had the writer's likes, dislikes, and his observations, always with a special flavour in humour, sympathy, aversion, style, charm, even oddity.'[6]

In 1926, Narayan joined the Maharaja's College under the University of Mysore as a BA student. It was in college that Narayan got his first taste of Shakespeare. Much of the credit went to Professor JC Rollo, who was well known all over South India for his

Shakespeare scholarship. His histrionics enchanted the boys, Narayan among them, as he paced up and down the halls reciting the monologues. He could make Shakespearean characters come to life with his animated and exciting lectures. To Narayan, Professor Rollo was an ideal teacher. After Rollo died in 1977, Narayan paid a glowing tribute to his former teacher in *The Literary Criterion*. He wrote he owed his 'love of English language and literature entirely to Professor Rollo.'[7]

And then there was Professor Toby who taught Greek drama and Victorian poetry. He was in every way a sharp contrast to JC Rollo. He had a peculiar accent and never made eye contact with the students. The boys joked that for many years he was under the fixed impression that he was teaching a class of girls, because all he saw in front of him was the end of their *dhoti*s which he mistook for skirts. Many years later, Narayan saw him in Leeds when he took a trip to the house of the Bronte sisters. As always, his eyes were fixed on the ground. Before his ex-pupil could hail him, he vanished.

In at least two letters to Graham Greene, Narayan would identify the early 1920s as the defining moment in his life and the starting point of his writerly life.

BECOMING A WRITER
A LEAP OF FAITH

According to Narayan's biographers, 'A Night of Cyclone', written in 1929, is his earliest datable short story. It was written in Vishakhapatnam, where Narayan and his younger brother were vacationing after his university exams. This was, however, by no means Narayan's first attempts at writing something serious.

He had started writing in his pre-college days, as confirmed by himself in *My Days*, 'mostly under the influence of events occurring around me in the style of any writer uppermost in my mind at the time.'[1] Around this time—this must be the mid-1920s—Krishnaswami had lost a dear friend that seemed to affect him much. Moved by his father's grief, Narayan wrote a 10-page prose piece called 'Friendship'. The language flowed like poetry and the lamentations, Narayan himself suggests, echoed Shelley's 'Adonais'. Narayan read it out to Srinivasan, but hid it from his elder brother whose sharp critical eye he feared. Nonetheless, he was proud of the piece; he carried it in his pocket and read it aloud to a few friends sitting by the Kukanahalli lake. Narayan described the episodes with wonderful humour in *My Days*. Whenever I could afford it, I gave them a cup of coffee at a restaurant on Hundred Feet Road. The cup of coffee blunted the listeners' critical faculties and made them declare my work a masterpiece.'[2] Some friends reacted by saying that it moved them to tears.

The next piece Narayan wrote was titled 'Divine Music'. It was composed on a bench by the Kukanahalli lake, almost in a state of trance. It was a meditative piece that didn't make much sense to its author even then, but he was sure it would be a treasured addition to world literature. Srinivasan and the inner circle of friends, high on caffeine, endorsed the author's views. Buoyed by the encouragement, he wrote a third piece which was even more abstract and obscure.

Narayan soon got the pieces typed out from Venus Typewriting Institute at Lansdowne Bazaar for two annas a page after he somehow managed to convince the typist that those were waiting to be published from London. He was not lying. He could convince the typist only because in his heart of hearts, he himself believed that his essays would soon be published in *The London Mercury* or *The Times Literary Supplement*. He borrowed money from his mother and posted them.

Then began the unnerving task of waiting for the postman on days when the foreign mails came. Day after day after day, the postman, Antony, waved at him from a distance and said, 'No letters for you', until one day there was a letter for him. 'I trembled as I took the packet…The sun beat down and blinded me…but I had no patience to wait till I reached my room…I stood in the shade…and ripped open the envelope, still hoping for a warm letter or a cheque to fall out; but a neatly printed rejection slip was pinned to the manuscript, which otherwise showed no sign of having ever been looked at.'[3]

The young aspiring author, who was supremely confident of the merit of his piece (when one of his brothers asked what it meant, Narayan had said its meaning could only be felt and not explained) took the rejection as a personal affront and went into a temporary depression. As soon as he recovered from it, he sent not one, but three manuscripts, to a different editor, Ellis Roberts of *Life and Letters*. There were classics like *The Vicar of Wakefield* that had been rejected by as many as

10 publishers, he told himself. Roberts, however, never got back to him.

***

Narayan received his graduation degree in 1930. It was delayed by a year by the fact that in his first attempt, he had failed in history. When the news of the failure reached him in Vishakhapatnam, neither the student nor his parents were much bothered by it. He simply had to take the history examination all over again. He finally did clear the paper and according to RK Srinivasan's diary, it was on 28 March that both of them learnt from their father that they had graduated. The convocation was held on 16 October 1930.

As soon as he graduated, a new burning question presented itself, which was, what he should do with his life next? There were different suggestions from different relatives and friends. Somebody suggested that he became a lawyer, somebody suggested a civil servant. Narayan himself thought about pursuing an MA degree in literature and becoming a lecturer. He had, in fact, made up his mind. The day he went to college with an application for admission to the MA class, his friend

MN Parthasarathy met him halfway up the stairs and somehow convinced him that pursuing a postgraduate degree in literature was the most certain way of losing interest in it. The advice struck a chord with Narayan and he decided not to go ahead.

But at the same time, it was unthinkable that one should stay home without doing anything after graduation. Inevitably he had to start sending out job applications and meeting influential persons known to his father. The first one of this lot was the Chief Auditor of railways who had been an old friend of his father. Krishnaswami was confident that he would help his son find a job in the railways. One morning, neatly dressed, Narayan went to meet him, already imagining himself as a railway officer, commanding stationmasters and travelling in luxury cars all over India free of cost. When Narayan explained his mission, the man wanted to know what subjects he had studied for his BA. When Narayan said history, economics and politics, the man looked at him disdainfully and said it would be impossible for him to find a job in the railways. The conversation lasted a few seconds, after which he waved Narayan off.

The next man Narayan met was another old friend of Krishnaswami who had retired from bank service.

Though Narayan never took interest in numbers and figures, he still went to see him, as desired by his father; once again, neatly dressed and thinking of himself as a bank officer. The bare-bodied man was fanning himself with a hand fan sitting on a swing when Narayan went and met him. The passage where Narayan describes this meeting in his autobiography is nothing short of hilarious: 'It was difficult to carry on a conversation with him as he approached and receded on his swing. I had to adjust my voice in two pitches to explain my mission and also step back each time the swing came for me.'[4] Like the previous fellow, this man too seemed to hate the subjects the job aspirant studied in college. He must pass book-keeping and accountancy if he wanted a bank job, he told Narayan. The conversation ended right there.

Meanwhile, Krishnaswami had retired from service and it was not easy to run a large family from his meager pension. The Narayans soon shifted to Laxmipuram to a smaller house. In his autobiography, Narayan remarks that the years spent at Bojjanna Lines were the dreamiest time of his life. The only happy thing about the house at Laxmipuram was that their neighbour was a pretty girl who could be seen through the window busy in her studies. She was never distracted by onlookers. When she won first class in several subjects in her BA examination and received medals, neither Narayan nor his brother was least surprised.

It was around this time that a monstrous Smith Premier typewriter that Seshachalam had gifted Narayan caught his attention. He placed it on the top landing of a wooden staircase in his new home. It was a magnificent machine which looked like modern-day computers and had separate keys for capital and lower cases. The entire staircase shook when it was in use. One afternoon, sitting on the landing, Narayan wrote a play called 'Prince Yazid'. It was the story of a Mughal prince tortured by his father. Srinivasan, younger brother and constant companion, helped Narayan type *My Days*. Narayan writes, 'If I'm not mistaken, he was the only reader' of the play.

Narayan makes it clear that his desperation to write something worthwhile was less of a creative pursuit and more caused by his earnest desire to help the family monetarily. He still had three younger brothers at school. Srinivasan was in his MA class. A few months later, with nothing to do in Mysore, Narayan moved to Bangalore and stayed with his grandmother.

To be back under her care was a *deja vu*. Like in those childhood days, he again had the freedom to roam about the streets of Bangalore, 'dreaming and thinking and planning'. Then one day in September, chosen by his grandmother as an auspicious time (according to his biographers, it was the Vijayadashami day), Narayan bought an exercise book and wrote the first line of what he planned as a novel, which went on to become *Swami and Friends* (this incident is mentioned in greater detail in the chapter 'Malgudi: An Imaginary Homeland').[5]

This was the beginning of a most remarkable journey.

Another important development happened around the same time. His father's untiring efforts to get him a job proved successful and Narayan joined the government school in Chennapatna, where his father had once been the headmaster. Narayan was happy to be able to relive his heady childhood days, and everybody in the family was ecstatic because, after all it was Chennapatna, the family's former hometown, and not far from either Bangalore or Mysore. The ecstasy was, however, short-lived.

On 1 December 1930, Narayan arrived at Chennapatna and drove straight to the school to join his new assignment. He was sent to a sixth standard class where he had to teach Tennyson's 'Morte d'Arthur'. An old staffer who had been there in his father's days kept reminding him of the expectations he had already set just by being Krishnaswami's son. His tone was the same as it used to be when Narayan had been a child. He had no idea how to teach, but somehow managed to read and explain 20 lines of the poem. The rest of the class was spent in silencing the boys and warning them of dire consequences if they came to school without copies or books.

Things took an undesirable turn the next day when the headmaster sent Narayan to the fifth standard to teach a physics class as the designated teacher was absent. Narayan's protestations yielded no result and he had to go. The boys were very rowdy and they couldn't care less about their new teacher. Then Narayan thought of a trick to placate them, but he had no idea that it would backfire. He asked the boys to write a composition on how they had spent their last vacation and told them they could leave after completing the task. Within minutes, around 50 exercise books were on his desk and the class was empty.

The next morning, as he was teaching Tennyson again, a peon brought a memo to be signed by Narayan.

When he read it, he found it was an official warning for him for letting go the fifth-form boys the previous day. 'If there is any repetition of such an act, the matter will be reported to higher authorities,' it said. It was to be kept in his service book. Narayan flatly refused to sign it and rushed to the headmaster's room after the class. A nasty and heated discussion followed. Narayan eventually signed the document in a fit of rage and asked for 15 days' leave on the second day of his job. When the headmaster denied him a long leave, he was further infuriated and said he was going away and 'you may do what you like.'

An hour later, he packed everything and boarded a bus for Mysore. The only student Narayan remembered from his teaching days was a tall boy called Anweruddin. He had caught his teacher's attention for all the wrong reasons; for not having the English poetry book with him and then refusing to read out from it. Anweruddin saw him at the bus stop and asked him where he was going. 'To Mysore. I am not coming back. Go and tell your headmaster that you saw me go away,' Narayan told him. The boy looked unhappy and stood next to him dolefully. When the bus came, he helped his teacher lift his luggage and bade him goodbye with a deep *salaam*.

Back home, he avoided facing his father for the first few days, until the day he was summoned in the hall and asked to go back to Chennapatna. In the friendliest tone he had ever heard his father speak in, Krishnaswami told him that he had spoken to the right people (possibly referring to Mr Wadia, a friend and director of public instruction) and Narayan would be treated well this time. He had also arranged an accommodation for his son where he was sure Kunjappa (Narayan's nick name in the family) would feel at home.

Narayan returned to Chennapatna, but perhaps he knew the job of a school teacher was not for him. To make matters worse, this time he was asked to oversee the drill session which was the last straw. The house where he put up was exactly the opposite of what his father had promised. He somehow spent a day and the next morning the idea of going back to school and coming back to that house horrified him. He left for Mysore again, this time, for good. It was the end of his teaching career.

Was Narayan temperamentally unsuited for a government job in a school, much like the Bengali poet Jibanananda Das who also quit his job as a lecturer in English at Delhi University and took a plunge into a deeply uncertain future? According to Narayan's biographers, if there was one thing that he craved, it was freedom—the freedom to choose what to do and when to do. Throughout his life, he loved his aimless daily walks. As a child, roaming the streets of Puraswalakam without a care in the world was his greatest delight. In his youth, he loved his sudden hikes to Chamundi Hill or solitary walks to the Kukarahalli lake. The two-year interregnum before and after college facilitated by failures in exams further whipped up his free-roaming spirit. He realised that only the life of a creative writer could give him the freedom he yearned for. Many years later, speaking to BBC radio, Narayan was to say,

> I chose to be a writer mainly because it is the only career which guarantees absolute freedom to live as one pleases, stay or go where one pleases without waiting for anyone's approval or sanction—freedom to sleep, read, walk and above all, turn towards one's work only at one's pleasure. This, indeed, is the meaning of the word freedom.[6]

At the same time, he knew that there was a price he had to pay for enjoying this freedom. Quitting a government job and choosing to become a full-time fiction writer, that too in English, was bizarre and unheard of in the 1930s, not only in Narayan's close circle, but in the entire country. There was no organised publishing industry in India to begin with. Then there was no one to look up to, and no market for Indian English novels either. But in his mind, he was certain. If he had to be something, he would be a writer. He had already taken the giant leap of faith.

RAJAM & THE MYSORE CITY REPORTER

Back in Mysore, Narayan had all the freedom he wanted. Most of the days, after his morning coffee and bath, he would take his umbrella and go out on a walk. At times he carried a pen and writing pad and sat down under the shade of a tree at the foot of the Chamundi Hills and wrote. On other days, he took out a cycle and rode for miles along the Karapur Forest Road and then sat on a wayside culvert and wrote. On days when he did not write, he simply sat and mulled over life and literature, watched farmers busy at work and the canals flowing past. He had very few demands of life and had no plans for the future. And that was exactly what he enjoyed. Not having to return home or report to anybody at a particular hour was a great luxury that he had always craved for.

Sometimes he returned home at noon for lunch, read for an hour or so, and then after a cup of coffee at 3, sat down to write. The delight of watching a novel grow in his own hands exhilarated him. Many years later, while writing his autobiography, he could not remember exactly how much he wrote every day, maybe 100 words or 1000, but to watch Swaminathan grow from a schoolboy to an adolescent was an unforgettable experience.

In *My Days*, Narayan says when he sat down with his pen, he did not have a plan for the forthcoming chapters. He only had a vision of how he wanted his central character, Swaminathan, to be. At night, he read whatever he wrote during the day, and stayed up well past midnight, making corrections and revisions. He himself realised how he was improving and how the narrative was galloping forward. Overall, it was a moment he had only dreamt of and was now living in.

As usual, the first person to read the manuscript was his younger brother Srinivasan. He became engrossed in the characters and made several observations. Then Narayan asked a neighbour, a friend called Purna, to read the pages and give his feedback. Purna was ecstatic. Meanwhile, the elders kept proposing various career opportunities. One of his father's friends proposed that he could join a newspaper. Narayan was firm in his stance. He said he wanted to finish his novel and when it would be published, that would solve all problems. Until then, everybody had to wait. The old man, as expected, was not impressed. Not only him, but practically everybody thought Narayan's plan for himself was impractical. Even he could not think of himself as an earning member of the family. But as long as his demands were nil, he thought nobody should complain. A few Gold Flake cigarettes, costing a couple of annas, were all that he needed for survival.

Apart from the novel, Narayan was also working on around 20 short stories at the time. He had plenty of material to work on. He listed the themes in his diary and whenever he needed a break from Swaminathan's narrative, he worked on the short stories. He made it a point not to base his stories around the theme of love. 'I wished to attack the tyranny of love and see if life could offer other values than the inevitable man-woman relationship.'[1]

Around this time, Narayan resumed sending his writing samples to editors. This time, of course, to the Indian ones. The result was more or less the same as before. The general response was that they lacked plot. He stayed in Madras for three months and pursued newspaper and magazine editors untiringly. Finally, his efforts yielded some success when he was asked to write a review of the book, *Development of Maritime Laws in 17th Century England*. Narayan had absolutely no interest in the subject matter but it gave him the opportunity to see his name in print for the first time. The same magazine also printed one of his short stories that paid him Rs 10. It was Narayan's first earning from writing. Next year *The Hindu* published a story and paid him Rs 18. The following year, another short story fetched him Rs 30.

Though he was trying to avoid the subject of love in his writing, the idea of love had quite captivated his mind. In *My Days*, he calls it 'a phase of impossible love-sickness'.

Maybe it had got to do with the amount of fiction that he was reading. Any girl who seemed to pay any attention to him captured his heart within an instant. This adolescent cry for attention didn't do him much favour until, much later, perhaps with a little more maturity, 'the real thing occurred'. He had been enamoured of a girl in a green saree who lived in the next street at Bojjanna Lines. Sometimes he followed her quietly until she reached her gate. He dreamed of the relationship maturing into a stage where he could propose marriage to her. Then one day, he lost sight of her and somebody else took her place. Narayan noticed this girl one day on his way to college. He kept looking for her every day subsequently. However, he also noticed that the girl would be 'ogling at' every passer-by and not only Narayan. So he lost interest in her soon and found a replacement—a girl who went to Maharani's College and often smiled as he passed her on the way.

Around the same time, Narayan even fell in love with a British doctor who had come to attend to his mother. His most serious infatuation was perhaps for a penfriend he had in England. They exchanged letters every week. She even sent Narayan her photograph, and he sent his. He would keep the photograph in his shirt pocket and hoped that she did the same thousands of miles away. All these were what Narayan calls 'false starts' in his autobiography.

Staying with his sister Janaki in Coimbatore in July 1933, one day Narayan caught a glimpse of 'a girl drawing water from a street tap, and immediately fell in love with her.'[2] According to prevalent social codes, he couldn't approach her or talk to her. The yearning only increased. Narayan later wrote in his autobiography that he was certain that he loved her. The girl's father, Nageswara Iyer, was a headmaster and friend of Janaki's father-in-law, and Narayan decided that he had to cash in on that. Moreover, the man was a book lover and loved to indulge in literary conversations. During one of these chats, Narayan gathered all the courage and suddenly broke off from the subject to make an announcement of his interest in his daughter. It was outrageous. Narayan writes:

> No one in our social condition could dare to proceed in the manner I had done. There were formalities to be observed and any talk for a marriage proposal could proceed only between the elders of families. What I had done was unheard of.[3]

The old man, however, did take it sportingly and explained to Narayan that it was not a decision that could be taken then and there. He said he had to consult his wife and the other women at home, Narayan's parents had to agree, and then finally, horoscopes had to be matched. A few days later, he asked the inevitable question, what he planned to do for a living. Luckily for Narayan, around that time, a small prose piece by him titled 'How to Write an Indian Novel' had been published in the well-known British weekly, *Punch*, and he was paid a respectable remuneration. This was, in fact, Narayan's first prestigious publication. It gave him a leverage to talk to his future father-in-law. He presented himself as a freelance writer who wrote not only for Indian magazines but also for London periodicals. He also explained to the old man that he was on the verge of finishing his first novel and it could bring him an income throughout his life. The man listened to him with much interest, but then said what many others had told Narayan earlier: couldn't his father get him a government job in Bangalore? As usual, this upset Narayan, but as usual, he was firm in his conviction that he could earn a living by becoming a writer.

The real obstacle was the horoscope. The headmaster consulted a few experts and came to the conclusion that his daughter and the young aspiring writer was incompatible. The boy had Mars in the seventh house; in other words, he was a *Manglik*, which meant marriage would spell doom unless the bride had the similar 'flaw'.

Despite everything, Narayan and Rajam got married on 1 July 1934 with all pomp and gaiety and exchange of gifts as desired by Krishnaswami and

Gnanambal. The groom was 28, the bride 16. No astrological difference or uncertainty over the boy's financial condition could come in the way of Narayan's single-minded zeal to marry the girl he was so deeply in love with. Even there, Narayan was a trendsetter. Love marriages were something extremely rare in those times and the youngsters in the family couldn't believe they were witnessing one.

From photographs that are available, one finds that Rajam was a slender woman, a couple of inches taller than her husband. She had an oval face and expressive eyes and thick black hair parted in the middle. In almost all the pictures, she wears a nose stud which stands out. Narayan's biographers point out that Rajam was actually embarrassed of being taller than her husband. So she made it a habit to walk a step or two behind him so that it did not become too apparent. Narayan, of course, couldn't care less. In RK Laxman's recollection, her sister-in-law was 'handsome, beautiful and tall', a beauty 'who moved like a swan.' Laxman's wife, Kamala, remembers Rajam looked like a Greek statue in a lilac saree.

As a daughter-in-law, Rajam became a part of the Mysore family seamlessly. Next to Narayan, the closest person to her at home was her husband's youngest brother, Laxman. At the time of the wedding, he was a 12-year-old school boy. Decades later, Laxman recollected to two of Narayan's biographers the day Rajam joined the family.

> She arrived with Narayan when I was in school. The 1 o' clock train or something like that. When I came back, I could see the whole house was different. There were decorations and flowers... My mother was sitting in a chair reading the paper. The daughter-in-law was sitting on the floor. I became shy. I thought, 'My God, what a thing has happened to my life.'

The same day after lunch, Laxman tiptoed to the new member in the family and showing a new sweater, asked for her opinion. When Rajam said, 'Very nice!', Laxman's confidence grew.

> Then I said, 'Please come into my room. I'll show you some more interesting things' ... And then we became very good friends. I became so fond of her, she was very nice. Then I went out

> on my bicycle and brought HK, my classmate, and told him, 'This is my sister-in-law.'[4]

In Narayan's own recollections, two things stand out about Rajam. One, she was very sensitive, and two, if needed, she could be very stubborn.

Within a few months of the wedding, Narayan's father suffered a cerebral stroke that left him paralysed. Since he was now bedridden, Gnanambal constantly had to be by his side. This increased Rajam's responsibilities in the house manifold. And she splendidly took over the burden of running the family. At the same time, it was now expected of Narayan to contribute more to the family income. Many authors in history, Rudyard Kipling, Gabriel Garcia Marquez, Ernest Hemingway, to name a few, have been journalists before they could establish themselves as full-time writers. Narayan, too, explored this route. And in 1934, he joined a propaganda newspaper called *The Justice* as its Mysore reporter replacing one of his college friends who had joined the Mysore Civil Service.

The Justice, founded in 1917, was the mouthpiece of an anti-Brahmin movement and was quite radical in its editorial stance. Narayan's assignment was just to report on the daily events in Mysore city. In the mornings he went news-hunting to the bazaar, the court, the police station and the municipal offices. At lunchtime he came back home and began typing out on an old Remington portable typewriter given to him by his sister whatever news he could gather. He was paid Rs 3.5 per column of 21-inch length. By 2:20 pm he had to reach the nearest post office and cable whatever he had typed.

After lunch and an hour's nap, he sat with Rajam and narrated to her all the important events of the day he had reported. Around this time, a short story, titled 'Dodu' (based on his younger brother Laxman) won the first prize in a literary competition organised by *The Merry Magazine*, and fetched him a substantial reward of Rs 250. It also encouraged him to regularly send his stories to the London-based publication. Soon it became a regular column. In his autobiography, Narayan admits that it was taxing for him to write light-hearted, funny stories week after week. But then, each story earned him a reasonable amount of Rs 50.

Meanwhile, as the Mysore city correspondent, he continued writing on topics of diverse nature. Murders were regularly reported. Narayan quickly learned the trick that journalists follow to this day: As long as there was abundant use of the word 'alleged' in crime reports, one was safe. Other than reporting on crimes and particular events, Narayan also wrote on matters that appealed to himself. For example, in the 16 February 1935 edition of *The Justice*, he reported on a debate held in Mysore where the motion was that in the opinion of the House, the growth of Kannada is hampered by Hindi propaganda. These were slightly controversial topics. And as expected, he soon ran into conflicts. The secretary of the local League of Nations Union, who was by profession a teacher of history, insisted on clearing stories written by all journalists before they could be filed. In his autobiography, Narayan narrates how he fought this unjustifiable intervention into his freedom of expression and the freedom of the press.

Hemavati was born in 1936. In 1939, with three published novels and a contract for a weekly column in *The Hindu* in his kitty, Narayan's life was going smooth, until a catastrophe struck. In January, Rajam and Hema had gone to Coimbatore. After three months, Narayan found it impossible to stay apart and wrote to Rajam asking her to come back to Mysore. On the day of their return, he received them at the railway station; little

Hema rushed forward and hugged her father. All the way on the horse cart, they talked and talked.

Three months later, on 6 June 1939, Rajam passed away after suffering from typhoid for a month. It was an unthinkable disaster for Narayan. Though Rajam was not keeping well for some time, he had not anticipated it at all.

> I felt clearly within my mind that I would never write a word again in my life. I had lost my anchorage. There was no meaning in existence. Dismal emptiness stretched before me. There were a hundred mementos and reminders each day that were deeply tormenting. I could not bear to stay in the room I had once shared with my wife…I found it impossible to wake up in the morning and get through the daily routine…I suffered from a horrible numbness…I avoided company.[5]

His weekly contributions to *The Hindu* stopped.

Narayan has chosen not to talk in his autobiography about the days leading to and following Rajam's death. Instead he has said,

> I have described this part of my experience of her sickness and death in *The English Teacher* (Narayan's fourth novel) so fully that I do not, and perhaps cannot go over it again. More than any other book, *The English Teacher* is autobiographical in content, very little part of it being fiction. The English teacher of the novel, Krishna, is a fictional character in the fictional city of Malgudi, but he goes through the same experience I have gone through and he calls his wife Sushila and the child is Leela instead of Hema, and the toll that typhoid took and all the desolation that followed with a child to look after and the psychic adjustments are based on my own experience.[6]

Something terrible happened in the morning of the day Rajam fell ill with typhoid. Egged on by his father-in-law, Narayan and Rajam had gone house-hunting in 1939. This is the episode with which *The English Teacher* begins. After rejecting a number of houses there was one that they liked. And it happened there. Rajam had gone inside the house on her own to check out the interior. When she didn't come out for almost 30 minutes,

Narayan went in looking for her and found that she was trapped inside a unclean lavatory, the door of which was freshly painted. In the novel, Narayan writes,

> Out she came—red and trembling, I looked at her and felt disturbed. 'What—What were you doing here?' I asked. She was panting with excitement. She was still shivering. I seated her on a stone slab nearby. 'What is the matter? What is the matter?' 'I went in there. The door was so bright and I thought it would be clean inside…but oh!' She screwed up her face and shattered, unable to bear the disgust that came with recollection… 'You went barefoot?' she nodded… 'I couldn't come out after I went in—the door shut by itself with a bang… Ah, the fly is another thing there!' She was convulsed with disgust. 'Oh! Oh! A fly came and sat on my lip.' She wouldn't bring her lips together. She kept rubbing them with her fingers in an effort to eradicate the touch of the fly.[7]

More than five decades later, Narayan confirmed to his autobiographers that the incident was very real. For days afterwards, Rajam would constantly rub her lips in order to get rid of the touch of the fly.

That very evening, Sushila in the novel falls ill, as did Rajam.

The novel contains a detailed blow-by-blow account of Sushila's suffering due to typhoid. If we consider Krishna's emotions as Narayan's, we get to know that sitting beside Rajam nursing her, he felt a strange kind of satisfaction at being close to his wife. He would often read out to her from the newspaper. Sushila/Rajam would whisper to him her willingness to get well soon. The novel charts Leela's reaction to her mother's illness as well as Sushila's parents' response to her daughter's plight. Dr Shankar, an eminent physician from Madras, (in reality, Dr Guruswamy Mudaliar) paid a visit, following which Sushila gets slightly better. The fever subsides. There is a brief moment of relief. Krishna goes out for a couple of hours. When he returns, Sushila is barely alive, breathing laboriously. Krishna stands like a statue as the physician pushes an injection as the last-ditch effort to revive the patient. An hour later, he shakes his head and says he has done his best. Sushila passed away around midnight.

There were suggestions from friends and relatives that Narayan should remarry. According to the author, those were more painful than the loss itself. There was another suggestion that he eventually took; he went to his sister's place in Madras for some time to get away from Rajam's absence in Mysore. Like in old times, he took long walks every day and avoided company as much as possible.

The other method that he tried was somewhat unconventional. In November 1939, his cousin Krishnamurthy took him to a veteran lawyer, Raghunatha Rao, who was known for his expertise into psychic experiments and conducting seances, where he could establish connections with departed souls. Initially Narayan had no faith in these spiritual/occult practices but he went. Once again, *The English Patient* describes these sessions in great details.

The particular method that Rao used was automatic writing. Narayan was greatly impressed when the medium announced that Rajam was in their midst. During cross-examination, she said a number of inaccurate things, but gave out exact details from a trip the couple had undertaken from Mysore to Bangalore a few years back. She even said she was very happy wherever she was and was keenly interested in the lives of her husband and daughter. Sleeplessness was the only reason to worry as far as her husband was concerned, she added. The first of these sessions were held on 29 November 1939. The second, on 6 December; the third on 20 December. There were over 20 sessions in total with Rao.

Narayan had preserved the pages on which words were written during the seance and made them available to his biographers decades later. Some of them were annotated by Narayan himself.

'NOVEL TAKEN. GRAHAM GREENE RESPONSIBLE'

These were the five words cabled to Narayan from Oxford by his friend Krishna Raghavendra Purna in 1935. These five words effected a turning point, not only in Narayan's life, but also in the history of Indian English literature. It would not be an overstatement to say that Narayan owed his literary life to Graham Greene. And theirs was a friendship that lasted a lifetime. There are instances in literary history of authors/poets being lifelong friends—Byron and Shelley, Eliot and Pound, Emerson and Thoreau, Tolkien and Lewis—but the camaraderie between Narayan and Greene was unique because it defied vast cultural and geographical differences and survived in letters for about two decades before they actually met each other.

Purna, a Mysore lad, had met Narayan, four years his senior, in 1920. When he left for Exeter College in 1931, he had promised the author that he would find his book a publisher. In this autobiography, Narayan says that he owes to Purna 'the consciousness that I am a writer'. Purna came from a reputable Mysore family and was, according to Narayan, an intelligent but 'too mild' fellow. At Oxford, he studied Modern History. He was immensely popular with his friends; a number of his contemporaries later told Narayan. In his political temperament he was left-leaning. When Narayan left his school job and returned home to become a writer, he was the first person to congratulate him. At Oxford, he fell in love with a young English woman, but due to reasons not clear to anybody, they never got married. That lady later met Narayan and Hema in Oxford, and they fondly talked about Purna.

It is possibly his leftist leanings that got Purna in close proximity to Graham Greene, who had been living in Oxford since 1933. At that time, Purna had in his possession at least 12 of Narayan's short stories and a play. One day he took these to Greene. In a letter to Purna, dated 1 December 1934, Greene wrote that he had finished reading the stories. And he thought that most of those were excellent; there was no reason why they shouldn't find a publisher. Then he went on to say an interesting thing. He felt many of those stories bore an influence of Chekhov more profoundly than many English writers. The interesting part is that till that point, Narayan had never read Chekhov. After Purna had sent the letter to Narayan, he made it a point to read the Russian author and found his short stories to be wonderful. Since Greene made this observation, almost every critic has drawn a parallel between Narayan and Chekhov.

The stories that Greene read included 'A Night of Cyclones', 'The One-armed Giant', 'The Two Brothers', 'Mother and Son', etc. One story that Greene liked in particular was 'Fellow Feeling'. The title was steeped in typical Narayan-esque irony. It is set in a railway carriage and tells the story of two passengers coming from rival castes. It was based on an incident Narayan had heard from his uncle Seshachalam many years ago. Since it talked about castes and animosity between them, Narayan had not sent this story to any publisher ever to steer clear of any controversy.

'A Night of Cyclones' was written when Narayan was still a student. 'The One-armed Giant' too was written in his college days. It had a beggar as its protagonist. In the introduction to one of his later collections of short stories, Narayan revealed that the story was based on a one-armed beggar who used to stand near the Bombay

Anand Bhavan Coffee House in Mysore when Narayan lived there in the 1920s. Greene, meanwhile, took so much interest in Narayan's short stories that he not only read and commented on them but also advised Purna on how to pitch them to publishers. In a letter dated 1 December 1934, Greene wrote that the volume of the stories taken together did not suffice for a collection. It would be better if three or four more stories could be added and then they could be sent to the publishers.

Greene even volunteered to write a personal note to Scott James of *The London Mercury* and Ellis Roberts of *Life and Letters,* recommending publication of these stories. He also had a backup plan in case these editors rejected them. Before sending them, he edited the stories and corrected the language errors, of course with permission from Purna.

Back in India, Narayan was still completely in the dark about all this. He had finished writing *Swami and Friends* in August 1932 and then didn't know what to do with it. A few of his short stories were getting published but there was no question of an English novel written by a relatively unknown author finding a publisher in India. He sent the manuscript to a number of British publishers, but to no avail.

> When I had completed the novel, I faithfully dispatched it to Allen and Unwin, and when it was returned to another publisher, and then another. I had got used to getting back my manuscript with unfailing regularity once every six weeks—two weeks onward journey, two weeks sojourn on a publisher's desk and two weeks homeward journey with a rejection slip pinned to it. All in all, it provided me with six weeks of hope. I had got used to this as an almost mechanical process and had shared all emotions surrounding a rejection.[1]

The last publisher Narayan decided to send the manuscript to was JM Dent & Sons in England which brought out the Everyman's Library Series. Presuming the outcome, Narayan had requested the editor to send the manuscript to Purna in Oxford, once it was rejected. In another letter to Purna, a dejected Narayan advised him to throw it into the Thames, once he received it. Purna, indefatigable, wrote back to his friend asking him not to despair and knocked on the doors of several publishers. When that didn't yield any result, he took it to Greene, as his last resort.

Greene found the novel absolutely delightful. He loved Narayan's objectivity; the total absence of authorial intrusions and comments. He found both of Narayan's first two novels remarkably mature and full of promise. In a letter to Purna in June or July 1935, the British author described *Swami and Friends* as an excellent piece of work on a par with the best of Narayan's short stories. Without wasting any more time, he had it sent to two publishers he personally knew. There was only one thing that concerned him, and that was the length of the novel. It had around 50,000 words and Greene thought 20,000 more would have made a perfect length, though he admitted that logically there shouldn't be anything such as 'the perfect length of a novel'.

In the 1937 introduction to *The Bachelor of Arts*, Greene has dwelt in detail on why *Swami and Friends* impressed him so much. He points out that till that point, his impression of India was based on the writings of EM Forster and Rudyard Kipling. Narayan, for the first time, offered him a first-hand account of Indian life. Quoting several sources, mostly Greene's 1990 work *Reflections*, Narayan's biographers write:

> For Greene, 'the story of a child written with complete objectivity, with a humour, strange to our fiction, closer to Chekhov than to any English writer, with the same underlying sense of beauty and sadness' always remained a favourite among Narayan's novels, '[A] book in ten thousand'. He came upon it at a time when he was dissatisfied with the subjectivity of contemporary English novelists. In reaction to the judgmental and moralizing objectivity of Victorian writers, they tended to state their point of view through becoming one of their characters, thus 'losing the clear line, the vivid visual graph of something observed from without'.[2]

Greene also savoured the fact that despite being written in pre-Independence India, *Swami and Friends* foregrounded Indian ethos, characters and culture, and relegated English characters to the blurry background. This, he thought with much amusement, would have irked Kipling quite a bit.

Purna's cable made Narayan ecstatic. 'I saw myself in a new role as a novelist. I could see the relief in my wife's face although she did not want to be too demonstrative about it.'[3] The first thing he did was to resign from his job at *The Justice*.

Greene wrote the first of over 100 letters to Narayan on 1 August 1935, where he addressed him as 'Mr Narayan Swami' and identified himself as 'a fellow novelist'. He informed Narayan that he had sent the manuscript to Hamish Hamilton and the latter had consented to publishing it. Founded in 1931, Hamilton was at that point of time one of Britain's most prestigious publication houses. It was later taken over by Penguin Random House. Greene even volunteered to talk to the publisher about the commercial and monetary aspects.

Days after Greene had met the publishers, Hamish Hamilton wrote to Narayan detailing the terms of the contract which covered two more books in future: 20 pounds as advance, 10 per cent royalty on the first 2000 copies and 12.5 per cent thereafter. The letter also proposed the name 'Swami and Friends' instead of 'Swami, the Tate', that Narayan had used initially.

The exchange of letters continued. On 11 August, in what should be Narayan's first letter to Greene from Mysore, the author wrote:

> My heart is so full at this moment that I can hardly say anything more than this...I can hardly believe that I am in a real world now. It took two years to write that novel and have been waiting for three years for it to be accepted by a publisher. I began to despair about a year ago... I hope I shall have a little freedom hereafter.[4]

In the same letter, Narayan told Greene that he had complete faith in him. 'I have absolutely no objection to have my English corrected by you. On the contrary, I shall feel honoured by it. You have suggested a change of title for the novel. I leave you free to give it any title you think fit. I shall be most happy to accept any terms that you get out of Hamish Hamilton,' he added.

About two weeks later, Greene wrote back to Narayan, this time with a rather unexpected request: instead of RK Narayana Swamy, the author should go with the name RK Narayan, he proposed. He cited the example of a German author, who he thought failed miserably because of his rather difficult name. Writing back to Greene, Narayan readily agreed to this suggestion as well. So, one might say that Narayan is indebted to Greene not only for his literary career, but also for giving him the identity with which the world knows him today.

In another letter, Narayan plainly put forward what he thought of Greene's contribution in his life. 'What you have done for me is the greatest service that one human being could do to another', he wrote.

Swami and Friends was published in London on 24 October 1935. Narayan was then 29. His joy knew no bounds. There was one glitch though. The first 50 copies had the author's name on the cover as 'RJ Narayan'. As is only to be expected of Narayan, he did not make an issue of it, and when he wrote to Greene expressing his pleasure, he did not even mention the error. In fact, decades later he admitted to his biographers that for a while he had even thought about changing his initials to RJ in order to avoid any unpleasant run-in with the publishers. Thankfully, he relented.

Though the response was not exactly electrifying, reviews were mostly positive. In the biography co-authored by Susan and N Ram, the biographers tracked down a large number of them. One reviewer lauded Narayan's delightful way of relating the life of a schoolboy. Another one pointed out that young boys would probably enjoy the novel. A review in *The Morning Post* on

3 December 1935, described the novel as 'unpretentious and extremely charming'. Another one in *The Spectator*, written by an Indian-origin writer, said *Swami and Friends* was indeed very good as a debut novel. 'I shall watch Mr Narayan's career with interest,' he remarked.

The review that delighted Narayan most was perhaps the one that appeared in *The Daily Mail* on 7 November 1935. The novel was described as a delightful story about life in an Indian school with equally vivid glimpses of life in Indian homes. A few reviews appeared in India as well. One in *The Hindu* in March 1936 said reading a book as delightful as *Swami and Friends* was a rare experience.

The novel, however, did not sell at all. Writing in his autobiography in 1974, Narayan held the timing responsible. '...It had no sales. It appeared in the company of record-breaking bestsellers such as *Man, the Unknown* (a book on psychology/anthropology by Nobel Laureate French surgeon Alexis Carrel) and *Inside Europe* (non-fiction by noted journalist John Gunther), and was simply flushed out of sight in the deluge'.[5]

This notwithstanding, the publication of *Swami and Friends* and Greene's exhortations led Narayan to write two more novels in the next two years: *The Bachelor of Arts* and *The Dark Room*. Narayan finished the first in March 1936 and the second by the autumn of 1937. Meanwhile, Hamilton had written to Narayan voicing its inability to carry on publishing his novels. It described the novel as a sad failure and expressed its fears that Chandran (the hero of Narayan's second novel) was going to do no better. Thomas Nelson,[6] the parent organization of present-day HarperCollins, published *The Bachelor of Arts*, once again, at the recommendation of Greene. Fittingly, Narayan dedicated this novel to the British author. It received a warm and encouraging response. Olivia Manning wrote in *The Spectator*,

> No foreign writer with so wide a gap to bridge between his world and his English readers has bridged it so successfully. From Sirajudowlla to the curious monsters of Mother India, the Indian male has been presented to the British female as a tyrannical horror, a nightmare in the home. Mr. Narayan has changed him for us into a human being.[7]

Twenty years later, Narayan met Hamilton in London at a gathering hosted by *The Spectator*. They both had a laugh over Hamilton's predictions about Narayan's novels going spectacularly wrong, and the British publisher saved the day by saying he would be forever happy at the thought of being Narayan's first publisher.

The Dark Room, one of Narayan's lesser-known but most masterly works, was published on 11 October 1938 by Macmillan. In a letter, Greene reminded him of the rich past of the publishing firm and the influence it had on the literary world. The reviews, too, were not only positive, but also in the superlatives, more often than not. Absorbing in its depiction of the Indian life—that's how the novel was described by none other than Somerset Maugham, who wrote to Narayan in December 1938.

So his first three novels had three different publishers. Not one to let go of this opportunity to make fun of himself, Narayan jumped into self-deprecating humour. 'One book, one publisher—and then perhaps he said to himself, "Hands off this writer,"' he writes in *My Days*.[8]

'It became a tradition for Narayan to send all his major fiction to Greene for an opinion before publication. For years, Greene edited the writing, cleaned up the grammar, supplied titles, and energetically sang his protégé's praises in the literary world.'[9] The correspondence stopped only during the early years of the Second World

War and began again in the second half of 1944. By now, Greene was working as the director of the publishing firm Eyre & Spottiswoode (which later merged into the present-day Methuen). Greene lost no time in telling his friend that his firm was planning to republish *Swami and Friends* and *The Bachelor of Arts.* Not only that, Greene planned the new edition of Narayan's first novel as an illustrated volume. Around the same time, Greene was also reading the manuscript of Narayan's fourth novel, the overtly autobiographical *The English Teacher.* He even suggested the title in place of the one thought of by Narayan himself, 'Our Jasmine Home'.

In one of the letters around this time, Narayan proposed the name of his youngest brother, Laxman, as the illustrator for the new edition of *Swami and Friends.* While Greene was open to the suggestion, he told Narayan that he had a second name in mind, the Polish artist Feliks Topolski. When Greene received samples of Laxman's work, he appreciated them much, but found them somewhat unsuitable for British tastes. Narayan, on the other hand, had no objection to going ahead with Topolski. In order to start working on the project, Greene asked for a copy of the book, since he thought his personal copy was somehow misplaced. It had the note: 'But for you, "Swami" should have been in the bottom of Thames now. RK Narayan Swami.' The copy is now preserved at the Boston University archives.

However, the plans for an illustrated edition somehow didn't see the light of day. Three decades later, when the Oxford University Press did bring out an illustrated edition of *Swami and Friends*, the artist was none other than RK Laxman.

In a letter dated 31 October 1945, Greene had written that he hoped to see Narayan one day in England, once the war was over. Eventually, Narayan met Greene for the first and last time in 1956, more than 20 years after they had started writing to each other.

When the Michigan University Press published Narayan's works in the mid-1950s, Narayan's readership grew steadily in the US. In 1956, after Hema had gotten married, he visited the country on a Rockefeller Fellowship. En route, he stopped in London and met Greene. The plot of *The Guide* was taking shape in his mind; in fact, he wrote the novel on this trip, mostly in Berkeley. As expected, he consulted Greene on its resolution—whether Raju should live or die. Greene is famously believed to have said that Narayan had on his hands 'the life of a man condemned to death before he was born and grown'.

MALGUDI
AN IMAGINARY HOMELAND

> I am often asked, 'Where is Malgudi?' All I can say is that it is imaginary and not to be found on any map... If I explain that Malgudi is a small town in South India I shall only be expressing a half-truth, for the characteristics of Malgudi seem to me universal.[1]

Apart from the last, all of Narayan's novels and most of his short stories are set in the fictional town of Malgudi. Like Gabriel Garcia Marquez's Macondo or William Faulkner's Yoknapatawpha country, it is the imaginary homeland for all of Narayan's unforgettable creations. It is, without an iota of doubt, the best-known fictional space in Indian literature. For millions of his readers, however, Malgudi is real, palpable, timeless and teeming with life.

In *My Days*, Narayan describes the moment of the birth of Malgudi thus:

> On a certain day in September, selected by my grandmother for its auspiciousness, I bought an exercise book and wrote the first line of a novel. As I sat in a room nibbling my pen and wondering what to write, Malgudi with its little railway station swam into view, all ready made, with a character called Swaminathan running down the platform peering into the faces of passengers and grimacing at a bearded face… (In the final draft, the only change was that the Malgudi station came at the end of the story.)[2]

In *Swami and Friends* there is a clear effort to mythicize Malgudi. Swaminathan would protest the allusion if it came from Mr Ebenezer, but there is, no doubt, an air of prelapsarian bliss in the town. The mythical river Sarayu flows through it.[3] People from all walks of life assemble on its sand banks in the evening enjoying a cool breeze, water lapping at their feet. Branches of *peepul* trees bow down over the stream and their leaves kiss the water. The rustle of leaves and chirping of birds fill the air.

The sight of the Sarayu on a moonlit night is Malgudi's pride. A little downstream, not far from the bank, is Nallappa's mango grove, where a herd of cattle can easily cross the river. Rajam and Mani, sworn enemies, arrive there for a predetermined duel, but end up becoming best of friends. Sitting by the Sarayu, Swaminathan feels 'perfect peace with the world'. River Sarayu is the heart of Malgudi, and it flows down in a rhythm of its own.

But it doesn't take much time for this picture of perfect bliss to be disturbed. The 1930s and '40s were tumultuous times in India with the struggle for independence at its peak. And what was happening in the rest of the country had its reflections and repercussions in Malgudi. In his very first novel, Narayan makes Malgudi the epicentre of the local nationalist movement.

Thousands of people from Malgudi assemble on the bank of the Sarayu to protest against the arrest of Gauri Shankar, a political leader in Bombay. The day was 15 August 1930. And Swaminathan experiences it first hand. While going to school, he sees a man clad in *khaddar* standing on a wooden platform and addressing a gathering. He narrates the travails of Gauri Shankar and exhorts the people to protest against his arrest. He reminds the gathering of India's heritage and the fact that this is a civilization much older than the English. There are things said that go over Swaminathan and Mani's head. But one thing that appeals to them is the fact that England, which is a nation no bigger than the Madras Presidency, is thousands of miles away, and yet is ruling India. The speech ends with '*Gandhi ki jai!*'. Swaminathan also joins the chorus.

The two boys are most intrigued by the speaker's statement that if every Indian spat on England, the country would drown. They fancy the idea. The eloquence of the speaker captures the young minds particularly when he appeals to everyone to boycott British goods, specially Lancashire and Manchester cloth and switch to *khaddar*.

In 1905, Gandhi had made the call to boycott foreign goods. When Mani points out to Swaminathan that his coat is made of Lancashire cloth, Swaminathan is not very convinced, but still so embarrassed that he wishes he came to school naked rather than wearing that coat. When the speech ends, it's already dark and a fire is lighted, where people throw their foreign clothes. As the flame whizzes, Swaminathan gets carried away and throws away his own cap. Next morning it dawns upon him that he has no cap to wear to school and if he wants a new one he has to approach his father. However, the protests turn violent the following morning and police resort to *lathi* charge.

In *Waiting for the Mahatma,* generally regarded as Narayan's most overtly political novel, the climate of Malgudi again becomes politically charged. The novel shows the arrival of Gandhi in Malgudi and many tenets of his political activism and philosophy—the Dandi March, the Salt Satyagraha, the advocacy of non-violence, struggle for swaraj—feature in it prominently. It is decided that Gandhi will be put up at the biggest and the most prestigious house in Malgudi, the Neel Bagh, in the upscale New Extension area, instead of the colonial-era Circuit House. After he addresses a large gathering on the bank of the Sarayu, Sriram, the protagonist, who lives on Kabir Street, an area of Malgudi that has doggedly resisted changes over centuries, becomes a follower of the Mahatma. The contrast between the resistance to change embodied by Kabir Street and the psychological transformation of the protagonist is one of the many instances of Narayan's brilliant use of his setting as more than just a geographical locale.

Scholars and enthusiasts trying to trace the origin of Malgudi over the years have mostly talked about its similarities with Mysore. But Malgudi can't be and isn't just Mysore. There are, most definitely, traces of Puraswalkam, Madras, Bangalore and even Coimbatore. This is a point Narayan's biographers make with conviction.

> Multiple images, experiences and influences could be expected to have their sway; quite which, transmuted by subsequent experience and by the creative process, would surface in a little town called Malgudi is not determined. What seems beyond dispute is that Puraswalkam, with its village traditions and small-town ambience, with its role of playing host to Narayan's most formative childhood years, could not escape making inputs into his fictional universe.[4]

Then again, writing to Greene in 1953, Narayan said they should meet in Madras and he would give the British author glimpses of the components that went into the making of Malgudi.

The name Malgudi too has intrigued readers over the years. Speaking to his biographers in 1985, Narayan explained the naming of the fictional town in a rather matter-of-fact manner:

> I was thinking of a name for the railway station. It should have a nameboard and I didn't want to have an actual name which could be found in a railway timetable. I wanted to avoid that because some busybody was likely to say, 'This place is not there. That shop he has mentioned is not there.' If it is a real town, it's a nuisance for a writer. I could as well have called it Trichy or Madurai or some name like that, but I wanted to avoid the known place that was listed. And while I was worrying about this problem, the idea came to me. Malgudi just seemed to hurl into view. It has no meaning. There is a place called Lalgudi near Trichy, and a place called Mangudi near Kumbakonam or somewhere. But Malgudi is nowhere. So that was very helpful. It satisfied my requirement.[5]

Then there are Narayan admirers from Bangalore who would make one believe, though without any evidence to back their claim, that Malgudi is a portmanteau of

Malleswaram and Basavangudi, two densely populated localities in the present-day IT hub of India.[6]

Malgudi is a town of real men and women. At the railway station, you might once run into the town's most famous inhabitant, the one-time tourist guide, Railway Raju. Exiting the station, Gaffur would be waiting in his taxi to take you on a city tour; first downtown towards the New Extension past Chandran's house and Rajam's; then uptown towards the Sarayu, past the statue of Sir Frederick Lawley, the military commander who had settled there after the mutiny. On your left, you can find the Albert Mission School. On the right, there would be the lawyers' colony, the police station and the court. If you go further up the Vinayak Mudali Street, you will find Nallappa's mango grove and then the river bank. Tucked away in a corner would be Margaaya, the financial expert's home. If you go westward on the south bank of the Sarayu, you can visit the village of the untouchables, where Gandhi stayed in 1937. Further down the street, there is the temple of Mangal. And if you do not want to take this route, you can ask Gaffur to turn right from Lawley's statue. Driving past the medical centre and crossing the Fountain Square, you will be in the market area. Further down the Market Road would be Welcome Restaurant and the Cooperative Bank. If you turn left before the restaurant, Sarayu Street will take you to North Extension.

One effective way of understanding what Magludi's cultural geography represents is to try and understand what is does not, that is, by defining it by its contradictions from alterity, or 'the Other'. Narayan facilitates this by making Malgudi a transitional site. There is the old town: the market area, Kabir Street or Vinayak Mudali Street; and there are the 'Extensions' (in today's parlance, they would be designated as 'New' or 'Greater'). The tension between these two locales captures the conflict between European modernity and Indian tradition, something that was unavoidable in late-colonial India, and defines Malgudi in terms of the values it seeks to hold on to.

Localities within Malgudi have their own characteristic identities. This is something that can't be said about Macondo or Yoknapatawpha or Hardy's Wessex. We are not only familiar with Malgudi's geography and topography, but also know each and every neighbourhood distinctly. Any attentive reader of Narayan would know the lanes, by-lanes and landmarks of Malgudi like they know their own hometown. Lawley Extension, a part of Malgudi Narayan returns to again and again, is one such area. It features most prominently in *The English Teacher*, where Krishna and Sushila go house-hunting. The name itself suggests that it's an upcoming locality—an extension of the old town that's the epicentre of Narayan's world. It embodies the changing face of Malgudi. The horrible experience that Sushila has behind the freshly painted lavatory door in the new house in Lawley Extension (narrated in the chapter 'Rajam') is perhaps Narayan's way of showing its inner bankruptcy and outer glitter. 'The impulse to extend is itself a challenge to the parameters of Malgudi's tightly circumscribed old town, which seems to comprise little more than the few streets clustered together around its focal point, Market Road,' writes John Thieme.[7]

A similar locale within Malgudi is New Extension, once again an upcoming neighbourhood. We get to live in it in *The World of Nagaraj*. Narayan brilliantly captures the challenges Malgudi faces from these Extensions in its bid to remain insulated from the unstoppable forces of modernity. When Nagaraj accompanies Gopu to New Extension in search of Tim, it's like a journey into *terra incognita* for him, though the locality is just a few miles from the old town. He is paranoid. Even the climate of the locality, which can be logically no different from Malgudi proper, seems alien to him. The typical Brahminical obsession with purity and cleanliness of Malgudi is absent here; so the narrow lane where they find Tim, a representative of the young generation with modern values, is filthy and disgusting. Nagaraj also observes that the place is full of 'junglees' who have come to work for the laying of railway tracks to Mempi Hills, and are threatening Malgudi's core values.

In sharp contrast to these, Vinayak Mudali Street or Kabir Street or Ellaman Street have preserved the quintessential Malgudi ethos, though they all also have their share of civic issues. Vinayak Mudali Street, where Margaaya, the protagonist of *The Financial Expert* lives, is close to the market area, the centre of the town, but is not as elite or aristocratic as Kabir Street, where Sriram of *Waiting for the Mahatma* lives. Margaaya's house, No. 14D, is known to everyone because his father was the first settler in the area, but two disadvantages that it has are its proximity to the crematorium and the open gutters next to it.

The other end of Vinayak Mudali Street is, however, a hallowed and important space in Malgudi's cultural geography with the Hanuman temple situated there. Raman in *The Painter of Signs* feels choked in Ellaman Street, which he sees as a wretched part of the town, though it is very close to Market Street and Kabir Street, the central business district. Though he is young, he is more at ease working in the tranquility of his backyard with the Sarayu flowing softly past it, than in the ever-so-busy humdrum of life on Market Street. 'Malgudi is, of course, far more than a physical locus. It is an episteme that incorporates numerous ways of perceiving India—social, spiritual, mythological and psychological among them—and in the vast majority of Narayan's novels these come together in the protagonist's consciousness, as he…struggles to find an appropriate dharma for his situation in life.'[8]

In her wonderful introduction to the 2006 Penguin edition of *Malgudi Days*, Jhumpa Lahiri says Narayan presented the bustling town—not only its demography but also its landscape—with the alacrity of a census worker. Malgudi, for Lahiri, '…is neither fully cosmopolitan, nor entirely agrarian, but somewhere in between, like most semi-urban centres in this country in the middle of the last century'. She further notes and marvels at the fact that Narayan has not only named the town, but also its buildings, bus stops, shops, restaurants and temples with such realism that the reader feels he frequents these places every day. Malgudi, Lahiri writes, is 'the sort of place that carnivals and expos pass through, the sort of energetic, idiosyncratic community that is increasingly rare not only in America, but all over the world'.[9]

Malgudi, then, is where we all belong, and where we all wish we lived.[10]

NOVELIZING INDIA

Narayan novelized India. I think there can be no better phrase to describe his oeuvre. Between 1935 and 1993, when Narayan's first and last novels were published, the socio-cultural idea of India had changed almost beyond recognition, and Narayan's fiction, subtly yet poignantly, strove to record that transformation.

John Thieme, in what is perhaps the most intellectually stimulating book-length critical work on Narayan, divides the 15 novels in three chronological phases. He classifies *Swami and Friends*, *The Bachelor of Arts*, *The Dark Room* and *The English Teacher* as 'Early Novels'. *Mr. Sampath—The Printer of Malgudi*, *The Financial Expert*, *Waiting for the Mahatma*, *The Guide*, *The Man-Eater of Malgudi*, *The Vendor of Sweets* and *The Painter of Signs* constitute the 'Middle-Period Novels', and are described by Thieme as Narayan's best achievements. The last four novels, written in the 1980s and 90s—*A*

Tiger for Malgudi, *Talkative Man*, *The World of Nagaraj*, and *Grandmother's Tales* are designated by Thieme as 'Late Novels'. It is commonplace in Narayan criticism to see the three phases as paralleling the four different stages of life according to the *Varnashrama* system in ancient and medieval Hindu culture—*Brahmacharya*, *Garhastha*, *Vanaprastha* and *Sannyasa*—with the early novels showing the protagonists' journey from the first to the subsequent periods.

Three of the early novels, barring *The Dark Room*, have often been called a trilogy. Taken together, they are what is called a bildungsroman in literary parlance—novels showing the growth of the protagonist's mind. The three protagonists, Swaminathan, Chandran and Krishna are a school-goer, a college student and a young English teacher respectively. There was a seven-year gap between *The Dark Room* and *The English Teacher*. This was personally and intellectually the lowest point in Narayan's life with his wife's untimely passing in 1938. The author took a really long time to recover from the tragedy and pick the pen up again. When he did, he produced the deeply meditative and autobiographical *The English Teacher*. Though all the three novels of the trilogy are autobiographical, this is almost a blow-by-blow account of Narayan's own life. The intensity of emotion that is on display here is not be found anywhere else in Narayan's writing.

The other element that is unmistakably present in all the early novels is the experience of life in a colonial setup. *Swami and Friends*, which has often been called out for its loose, episodic structure, is a decidedly anti-colonial novel. The clash of cultures, an unavoidable impact of colonization, creates a deep confusion in the mind of Swaminathan, as it did in the mind of an entire generation forced to dwell in a hybrid space. On the one hand, he takes part in colonial resistance—in trying to decolonize the mind by protesting against Mr Ebenezer's insult of Indian gods or in participating in the burning of foreign clothes—on the other hand he is keen to play cricket like the colonial masters; in fact, the very name Malgudi Cricket Club (MCC) reeks of colonial mimicry. Narayan subtly portrays Swaminathan getting caught between these two contradictory impulses and suffering from a sort of identity crisis that is faced by every colonial subject. He goes to the Board High School but is part of the Albert Mission School cricket team. And when these two schools face each other for a cricket match, his loyalties are split. He feels choked under the pressure of continually having to inhabit this hybrid space and simply runs away from life. He loses his way in a forest and wakes up with the yearning to go back to his Granny and her essentially Indian lifestyle. Narayan makes us realise that Swaminathan, though a typical colonial subject, is essentially Indian.

Even as Narayan portrays Swaminathan's trials and tribulations, he switches back and forth in his language as well. On the one hand, he uses the standardized English of his main narrative and on the other, the verbal Indianized English of his characters. The attentive reader will witness, in these pages, the historic moment of the birth of Indian English by one of its earliest exponents.

The Dark Room is an 'unexpected' novel, for all intents and purposes. Savitri, ironically named after the mythic wife in *The Mahabharata*, who is an archetype of wifely devotion, is a wronged wife who is emancipated enough to stand up to her bullying husband, but finds that she has nowhere else to go. In presenting his only female protagonist, Narayan momentarily shifts from the male point-of-view of his earlier and later novels and creates an unforgettable woman character who, though not as complex as Rosie or Daisy of Narayan's later fiction, has her peer in Ibsen's Nora and Tagore's Mrinal.

Their predicaments are remarkably similar, though their reactions to them are not. For the first time, Narayan was venturing into feminist territories and taking on patriarchy, and he was very clear in his mind with what he wanted to achieve in *The Dark Room*.

> I was somehow obsessed with the philosophy of Woman as opposed to Man, her constant oppressor. This must have been an early testament of the 'Women's Lib' movement. Man assigned her a secondary place and kept her there with such subtlety and cunning that she herself began to lose all notions of her independence, her individuality, stature and strength. A wife in an Orthodox milieu of Indian society was an ideal victim of such circumstances. My novel dealt with her with this philosophy broadly in the background.[1]

No wonder, Nilufer Bharucha found the novel ahead of its time.

Narayan, once again, defines Savitri by telling us what she is not; by establishing her alterity from a number of other female characters, Gangu or Janamma or Shantabai, for example. The first is an eccentric, the second an extremely submissive wife who believes it is a wife's duty to feel whatever her husband does and thinks is right, and the third, a newcomer to Malgudi, is someone who left her drunkard husband's home at 18. Faced with her domineering husband Ramani and the knowledge of his adulterous affair with another woman, Savitri withdraws into a dark room, both physically and mentally; it is an escape no doubt, but is it necessarily a better alternative? Narayan leaves that question unanswered. For a brief while, she explores another escape route—she takes up the role of an attendant in the village temple. But after spending one terrifying night in a dark room in the temple, she realises that it is not a possible alternative for her, and she returns to her marital home and to the role of wife.

It is almost unanimously accepted by Narayan scholars and readers that the middle period saw Narayan at the height of his abilities and two novels from this phase, *The Financial Expert* and *The Guide,* are considered his best by many. The protagonist of all the seven novels from this period is the quintessential common man in different avatars. They are in the second phase of *Varnashrama*, that is *Garhastha.*

The Financial Expert tells the story of Margaaya, a moneylender from Vinayak Mudali Street, becoming Malgudi's richest man. The character, Narayan later explained, was inspired by a peon who was dismissed from government office where one of Narayan's brothers once worked. Humiliated by an official of Malgudi's Central Co-Operative Land Mortgage Bank, Margaaya decides to take matters in his own hands, and starts a money-lending business under a banyan tree opposite the bank and establishes himself as a rival to the institution. Gradually, as he prospers, he starts to believe that money can solve all his concerns. He ignores the local priest's warning that Lakshmi and Saraswati are often rivals, and when one is pleased, the other may desert him altogether. This proves true in Margaaya's life and that brings about his tragedy.

Yes, at the surface level, the narrative has a strong moralistic tone that makes it akin to a fable. But Margaaya's tale stands out in Narayan's entire corpus because he 'both embodies and challenges traditional values.'[3] Coming from Vinayak Mudali Street, he suffers from a sense of inferiority and his pragmatic pursuit for wealth is as much habitual as a means to climb up the social ladder. This pursuit results in a clash between his assigned role in the Tamil Brahmin society and his moneymindedness and entrepreneurial zeal. He challenges the tradition embodied by his contemporaries, that is, some of the other protagonists, Sriram of *Waiting for the Mahatma*, Srinivas of *Mr Sampath* or Nataraj of *The Man-Eater of Malgudi*.

The Guide, the novel that made Narayan a household name outside the literary world through its film adaptation that starred the matinee idol, Dev Anand, belongs to this period. *The Guide* is the story of Raju. He is the centripetal force around which all the other characters and incidents revolve. The novel spans Raju's career—from his childhood to Railway Raju, to Raju the guide, Raju the illicit lover, the impresario, Raju the forger, the prisoner and ultimately, Raju the fake *sadhu*. This is the path that the novel walks. But that does not mean he is the only moving force in the novel. In *The Guide*, Narayan creates his most unforgettable female character, Rosie. She is not the conventional conservative upper-class Hindu woman we are used to seeing in Narayan's novels. She is not like Savitri. Narayan makes that apparent in the name itself, as he does for Daisy in *The Painter of Signs*.

Rosie is the daughter of a *devadasi*, but she refuses to be identified by the circumstances of her birth. She has a Master's degree in Economics and she is a danseuse. Dreaming of climbing up the social ladder, she marries Marco, supposedly a Western man, liberal and ambitious. But he turns out to be the exact opposite. He is cold and unfeeling like the stones he excavates for a living. He refuses to recognize her talent, and confines Rosie within the four walls of 'the dark room'. This is where Raju comes into the scene. He gives Rosie a completely new perspective of life. He is sensuous and warm, and he shows Rosie the promised land—a career in Bharatnatyam dance.

In a way, the novel is about Rosie's tragedy. Narayan wonderfully weaves the classic formula of a tragedy within the narrative. The reader cannot decide whether Rosie is rightly punished or is more sinned against than sinning. She is a sensitive, educated, graceful and talented woman; so the sense of loss at her fall is quite evident. But at the same time, she is an illicit lover, a seductress, a she-devil, a 'viper'. Even at the height of her fame, she feels a strong sense of regret for deserting her husband. But then, Marco did not want a wife, he wanted a servant. This ambivalence gives Rosie's tale an air of sensitivity and realism. And then, those who want to see the working of the principles of *karma* in Narayan's fiction, readily identify it in Rosie's tale.

The other significant feat that Narayan achieves in *The Guide* is in its narrative technique. He uses a braided narrative, weaving the first-person autobiographical confessional voice and the third-person omniscient narration. The narrative also moves back and forth in time throughout. The very first chapter gives the reader a microscopic vision of the entire novel by effecting a constant time shift. It begins in the present with Raju and Velan, then goes back to Raju's childhood and then comes back to the present with Velan bringing his sister to Raju, the spiritual guide. The reader finds an ex-convict out of jail being accepted as a *guru*! It instantly kindles her interest. And then the mention of the femme fatale, Rosie, stokes it even further.

Within this framework, there are multiple mini-narratives—those of Gaffur, Sait, Marco and so on. And there is also a mythical subtext that is buried in the novel. The attentive reader can find it in the motifs and symbols hidden in the text. It starts with Raju, who much like Krishna, is (re)born in the prison. Then there is the association of Rosie with the snake. She is called a viper, a cobra, a snake woman, the *Nagakanya* of Hindu mythology, the archetypal seductress. Is Raju, then, the helpless victim of a seductress' charms? Rosie is also a *devadasi* by birth, associated with the heavenly dancing girls like Menaka, who seduced Visvamitra. Does the subtext suggest that Raju is a victim of circumstances?

It is, then, not difficult to see why *The Guide* is considered by many as Narayan's maturest work. It fetched him the Sahitya Akademi Award in 1960. 'Nowhere else is his irony sharper or more firmly wedded to the moral imagination, nor has his technique been subtler,' writes MK Naik.[4]

The 'Late Novels' see Narayan's art on the decline. Thieme calls *The Painter of Signs* Narayan's last major novel. He wrote four more after that. They 'demonstrate a falling-off in his talents. Nevertheless, (they) develop interesting variations on several of the defining themes of his work, particularly the passage into the fourth stage of the *Varnashramadharma*…and the Hindu reverence for animal life and the natural world.'[5]

Until the lion learns how to write, every story will glorify the hunter, says an African proverb. *A Tiger for Malgudi,* perhaps the best work of this phase, allows the lion (the tiger in this case) to write, one could say. It can be read as a companion piece to the earlier *The Man-Eater of Malgudi*. In the earlier novel, Vasu, a taxidermist by profession, kills and stuffs a tiger in the attic of Nataraj, who is extremely reverential to animals, and doesn't even want to be seen killing a fly. Here, in *A Tiger for Malgudi*, the narrative is reversed, by making the tiger, Raja, the protagonist and humanizing him with qualities that are lacking in the human characters of the novel. By giving the tiger a voice, Narayan brings in issues that would be addressed today by scholars of eco-criticism and anthropomorphism.

In *Grandmother's Tale*, Narayan's last foray into the longer format, he returns to his roots, as it were. The novella is based on the life and times of his great grandmother as he had heard from his grandmother. As in *The English Teacher*, here also the line between fact and fiction gets blurred as Narayan seamlessly moves between the two. Thieme points out that many details from the author's recollection of his grandmother find place in this novella as happening in the great-grandmother's life. At one point, even incidents from his own recent life, completely unrelated to the novel's subject, make intrusions into the narrative, for example, his recent visit to 1, Vellala Street, where it all began more than half a century ago.

Other than these 15 novels, Narayan's reputation (though he never bothered about it much) rests largely on the over 100 short stories he wrote across roughly 70 years. As many as 10 volumes of short stories were published during his lifetime. Most of these were first published in *The Hindu* newspaper. In July 1969, the *Playboy* magazine published his story 'A Breath of Lucifer'. He was prolific compared to his contemporaries (Raja Rao produced only one volume of short fiction and Mulk Raj Anand produced five). This is because at his heart, Narayan was a storyteller. In the introduction to *Malgudi Days*, Narayan himself admitted that he enjoyed the short story form more than novels. He unabashedly says that the sheer task of writing 60,000 to 1,00,000 words made him feel restless and uneasy. He felt shackled. He then goes on to say:

> At the end of every novel I have vowed never to write another one—a propitious moment to attempt a short story or two. I enjoy writing a short story. Unlike the novel, which emerges from relevant, minutely worked-out detail,

> the short story can be brought into existence through a mere suggestion of detail, the focus being kept on a central idea or climax.[6]

In the same essay written in September 1981, Narayan also defines what counts as material for a short story for him. He discovers a short story, he says, 'when a personality passes through a crisis of spirit or circumstances.'

A keen observation of life, lively characters, realistic plots, a fine blend of subtle humour, irony and wit and a simple, effortless language that tugs at the heartstrings are hallmarks of Narayan's short fiction as much as of his novels. In addition, what makes the short stories particularly enjoyable is a strict economy of narration. Never one to overstate things, Narayan makes this primary requisite of short stories work to his favour and proves himself a master of understatement. One can find examples on almost every page of Narayan's short fiction. In the story 'Lawley Road', he talks about the municipal drive to rename the city's parks and streets. He writes,

> They made a start with the park at the Market Square. It used to be called the Coronation

> Park—whose coronation God alone knew; it might have been the coronation of Victoria or of Asoka. No one bothered about it. Now the old board was uprooted and lay on the lawn, and a brand-new sign stood in its place declaring it henceforth to be Hamara Hindustan Park.[7]

In a show of fine authorial judgement, he resists from commenting on the judiciousness of the name change. Just the phrase 'declaring it henceforth to be' suffices for him.

In 1986, *Malgudi Days* became a nation-wide phenomenon and a household name when a TV series based on Narayan's stories was telecast on Doordarshan, the national TV channel; 13 episodes in English and 54 in Hindi. To the children of that generation across the length and breadth of this country, *Malgudi Days* on TV brought unadulterated joy and innocent pleasure. Directed by Shankar Nag and with music scored by veteran Carnatic musician L Vaidyanathan, the show was based on stories from *Malgudi Days*, *A Horse and Two Goats*, *An Astrologer's Day*, as well as episodes from *Swami and Friends* and *The Vendor of Sweets*. In 2006, the series was revived and 15 new episodes were made by director Kavitha Lankesh.

It is worth remembering that when Greene compared Narayan to Chekhov, he did so on the basis of his reading of his short stories. It is a bit of a surprise that John Thieme does not mention Narayan's short fiction at all in his book. MK Naik pays some attention to it in *The Ironic Vision: A Study of the Fiction of R.K. Narayan*, though his comments are not always favourable.

Narayan's signature witticism and humour are more abundantly on display in his nonfictional writings than in his fiction. The reasons for this could be many. In his essays, he could address the readers directly and without the limitations imposed on him, while writing novels or short stories, by the requirements of a well-knit plot and the demands of realism. And Narayan, as we have already noted, loved the shorter format dearly. His struggles with word count began with his very first novel, which at 50,000 words fell short by 20,000, according to his agent. In his nonfictional writings, none of these mattered, and Narayan was at his playful best.

The best of Narayan's nonfictional writings can certainly be found in his autobiography *My Days*. There isn't a single dull moment in the recollections as humour and pathos go hand in hand. Anecdotes, confessions, reflections and musings of various kinds colour the pages of the book and the language, like in all of his writings, easily melts the reader's heart. Towards the end of the book, Narayan describes his present life thus:

> I find every excuse to drive 120 miles over a mountain road to visit my daughter and spend an unspecified number of days… (to) enjoy my grandchildren's company. My granddaughter would resent being called a grandchild now. When I was writing *The Man-Eater of Malgudi*, she was at the stage of squeezing herself beside me in my chair and carrying on an undertone conversation with her doll… Today she is a high school girl interested in Enid Blyton, film music over the radio and Malgudi tales. Some months ago, she set up a model of Malgudi with miniature streets and buildings. My grandson is 11 years old and exact copy of Swami in *Swami and Friends*... He's a very busy grandson, totally absorbed in his school politics, homework, cricket team, cycling and ping pong.[8]

Apart from the autobiography, *A Writer's Nightmare* contains some of Narayan's finest and wittiest non-fictional writings. It is a collection of personal essays written over 30 years from 1958 to 1988 for his Sunday column in *The Hindu*. In the introduction, Narayan expresses his fondness for the personal essay as opposed to what he calls objective essays. 'I have always been drawn to the personal essay in which you could see something of the author himself apart from the theme... it (has) the writer's likes, dislikes, and his observations, always with a special flavour of humour, sympathy, aversion, style, charm, even oddity.'[9]

A MYRIAD-MINDED MAN

In September, 1964, Narayan received a letter at his Yadavgiri home from New York. The sender wanted to meet the author for acquiring the film rights of his novel *The Guide*. His name was Dev Anand.

Narayan's response to and recollection of the entire episode relating to the filming of *The Guide* gives us a sneak peek into the mind of the man. Not only was he thoroughly unimpressed, he actually felt what happened in the process was 'ludicrous and even tragic'. After the customary exchange of pleasantries, the actor-producer of the soon-to-be made film brought out a cheque book and asked the author to quote any amount he felt he deserved. Narayan felt numb for a few moments and then quoted a 'modesty reckonable' amount as advance and a small percentage on the profits that the film would make. What he told Dev Anand tells us a lot about the character of the man. 'Let me rise or sink with your film. I do not want to exploit you.'[1]

What irked Narayan most was that the film was to be set not in Mysore or anywhere else in South India, but in Jaipur, which is, in his own words 'as distant from Malgudi as perhaps Iceland.' This, after the author had actually taken the trouble of taking the film crew around Mysore to point out places that might have gone into the creation of Malgudi. When he demanded an explanation for the shift, he was told that Malgudi didn't exist anyway. Narayan felt greatly humiliated at this. 'By abolishing Malgudi, they had discarded my own values in milieu and human characteristics,' he writes in *My Days*. It is one of the rare moments in the book where he sounds really bitter. Apart from the change of locale, there were a number of other alterations made—from changes in the heroine's character to addition of scenes to placate financiers' whims—which Narayan could never come to terms with.

Then there was the dinner in Bombay where Narayan was invited to dine with Lord Mountbatten. The idea was that the Viceroy would be convinced to persuade Queen Elizabeth to attend the world premiere of the movie. To his utter astonishment, Narayan found that the veteran American author Pearl Buck, who wrote the screenplay, knew hardly anything about the story. Narayan narrates the episode in his signature humorous style, but the disappointment he felt is clear in his autobiography.

The entire *Guide*-ruckus shows how sensitive Narayan was about his creations. Neither a blank cheque, nor the glamour of Dev Anand and Waheeda Rehman, and not even the promise of nation-wide popularity by dint of the film could make up for the sense of waste he felt at his novel being violated by the filmmakers.

This uncompromising attitude towards his own creations landed him in further trouble in the US when he refused to give permission to a stage adaptation of *The Guide* by Harvey Breit, the then literary editor of *The New York Times.* In the version that he wrote for the stage, the character of Rosie did not exist. And then, there was a scene where the hero would be seen urinating on the stage. Breit was a long-time friend; still Narayan was firm in his decision. Within days Narayan's lawyer informed him at the Chelsea Hotel in New York that Breit had sued him. He suggested Narayan leave the country at once before he is summoned and a long drawn legal process gets underway.

At his wit's end, Narayan packed his bags within an hour and roamed the streets of NY throughout the day, 'like a criminal on the run' to avoid getting caught by the court summoner. His friend Natwar Singh, a foreign service officer in the US then and later the Minister of External Affairs of India in the Manmohan Singh cabinet, came to his rescue. The summons did reach him at his Coimbatore residence weeks later. Eventually, the court gave the verdict in his favour.

In his recollections of RK Narayan,[2] the veteran diplomat and politician describes the author as 'one of the most comfortable persons to be with'. Singh had first heard of Narayan from EM Forster. On a May afternoon in 1954, sitting at Cambridge, the British author strongly recommended Narayan to Singh because his novels have 'high-class comedy, without any-isms'. A year later, on an official trip to Mysore, Singh found his way to the author's Yadavgiri home. Opening a wooden gate and walking a few steps on a grovel path, Singh found the man standing in a shirt and a *lungi*. That is how and when their friendship began.

In March 1961, Narayan visited Delhi for the first time in his life to receive the Sahitya Akademi Award. When Singh asked how he could help, Narayan requested him to arrange a meeting with Prime Minister Jawaharalal Nehru. At Teen Murti Bhavan, Narayan presented him his latest novel, *The Man-Eater of Malgudi*. Nehru said his daughter had read many of Narayan's novels with much interest, and so did one of his nieces who is a writer (referring, of course, to Nayantara Sehgal). Nehru was shocked to learn Narayan had never been to Delhi before. In characteristic composure, Narayan replied, 'My writing keeps me busy in Mysore and I had no particular reason to come to Delhi.'[3]

When *My Days* came out, Singh was surprised not to find any mention of the meeting. How could an author, or anybody for that matter, forget to mention his meeting with the Prime Minister, that too a man like Pandit Nehru, in his autobiography! On being asked, Narayan said, 'It never occurred to me to give publicity to it, and in any case I could not weave it into the narrative. *My Days* is a literary work, not a political tract.'[4]

Modesty, Natwar Singh felt, was Narayan's middle name.

Apart from literature, gardening and studying about plants gave Narayan much pleasure. He inherited this love from his grandmother. The home he built for himself at 15, Vivekananda Road, Yadavgiri, was surrounded with greenery. The reason Narayan selected that 'underdeveloped' and 'desolate' spot on the outskirts of Mysore was because there was a large frangipani tree in full bloom standing on the edge of the plot. Begun in 1948, the house took five years to be completed. Even after that, Narayan divided his time between the family's Laxmipuram home and his new house. His favourite part of the house was a large round hall on the first floor with eight windows offering a view in every direction—the Chamundi Hills—vast stretches of green meadows and a rail line far away near the horizon. The cacophony of a variety of birds perched on frangipani branches kept him company as he enjoyed his favourite curd rice and coffee, or chewed his *paan* or relished his favourite desserts.

Coming back to his interest in gardening, Narayan says he fancied himself as a horticulturist. He knew everything about plants, fertilizers, soil management, etc. He listened to radio talks on farming with keen interest. In the eagerness to actually indulge himself in agriculture he later acquired a piece of land on a hillock on the outskirts of Bangalore. The experiment, however, did not succeed.

In 1985, Narayan was nominated to the Rajya Sabha, the upper house of the Indian Parliament. In his maiden speech in the House in 1989, he spoke on the need for children to have a balanced life between homework and play; in particular, on the weight of schoolbags. He asked for the abolition of the practice of carrying schoolbags, if necessary, by an ordinance. He said,

> I have investigated and found that an average child carries strapped to his back, like a pack-mule, not less than six to eight kgs of books, notebooks and other paraphernalia of modern education in addition to lunch-box and water bottle. Most children on account of this daily burden develop a stoop and hang their arms forward like a chimpanzee while walking, and I know cases of serious spinal injuries in some children too. Asked why not leave some books behind at home, the child explains it is her teacher's orders that all books and notes must be brought every day to the class, for what reason God alone knows…

> Other areas where the child needs protection is from involvement in adult activities such as protest marches, parades, or lining up on road-sides for waving in VIPs; children are made to stand in the hot sun for hours without anyone noticing how much they suffer from fatigue, hunger and thirst. Children must be protected, and cherished which would seem especially relevant in this year of the Nehru centenary.[5]

The Times of India reports that his speech led to the formation of a committee led by the educationist Professor Yash Pal to look into the matter.[6]

Soon after completing *The World of Nagaraj*, Narayan fell ill and shifted to his daughter's home in Madras. In 1994, Hema died of cancer. For the rest of his long life, the author was looked after by his granddaughter Mini. In the last 20 years of his life, Narayan found a trusted friend in N Ram, the publisher and editor of *The Hindu*, and his future biographer. Ram spent the late evenings with Narayan discussing myriad issues till well past midnight. Ram, the author, and the latter's son-in-law Chandrasekhar formed what Narayan preferred to call a night club. Ram recollects:

> Narayan did not like anything that was extravagant or sentimental... Narayan valued friendship more than anything else. Friendships and people who did not change over decades, over different eras, different locations, different settings, fascinated him.[7]

One of his last meetings with journalists (one cannot call it an interview since he met the reporter only on that condition) was with Swedish scribe Zac O'Yeah. O'Yeah read *The Guide* and *The English Teacher* in Swedish translation and travelled half across the globe to meet the Indian author. When he called up the author's home, he was told by his nephew that the author did not give interviews. When O'Yeah said he was an ardent admirer of Narayan, the author agreed to meet him, but without a tape-recorder or a note pad. 'He took a decision not to give any more interviews,' O'Yeah writes, 'after a photographer from *Time* magazine had dragged him around the city, and finally got him to pose on the beach in Chennai. Subsequently he had to spend 10 days in a hospital recovering from heat stroke, only to find to his dismay that the magazine had used one small picture, the size of a postage stamp.'[8]

***

Narayan dedicated his last novel, *Grandmother's Tale*, to his late daughter. He dictated the Foreword to Ram days before the novel's publication. It gave him a lot of satisfaction. On 1 May 2001, he was hospitalized in Chennai with cardiovascular problems. Hours before he went into ventilation, he asked Ram to get him a new diary so that he could write something new, but that was not to be. The voice of India with a southern accent fell silent on 13 May 2001, after living a full life, comforted by the impregnability of his reputation. Narayan, however, couldn't care less.

ENDNOTES

Introduction

1. Meenakshi Mukherjee, *The Twice Born Fiction: Themes and Techniques of the Indian Novel in English* (New Delhi and London: Heinemann, 1971), p. 20.
2. Came out serially as 'Wife' in *Indian Field* founded in 1859 by Kishori Chand Mitra, the brother of Peary Chand Mitra who wrote the first Bengali novel *Alaler Ghorer Dulal.*
3. See Supriya Chaudhari, 'Beginnings: *Rajmohan's Wife* and the Novel in India,' in *A History of the Indian Novel in English,* ed. Ulka Anjaria (New York: Cambridge University Press, 2015), pp. 31–44.
4. M. K. Naik, *A History of Indian Literature in English* (New Delhi: Sahitya Akademi, 2009), p. 168.
5. Susan Ram and N. Ram, *R. K. Narayan: The Early Years, 1906–1945* (New Delhi: Viking, 1996), p. 93.
6. '*Dayadhvam*' or 'be compassionate' is what he instructed the demons among his students; to the gods his said, '*Damyata*' or 'control yourself'; and to the humans he said '*Datta*' or 'give'. In his commentary on the Upanishads, Dr Radhakrishnan says that all these three instructions are actually for human beings, as there are no gods or demons other than men. See S. Radhakrishnan, Introduction to *The Principal Upanisads* (New York: Harper, 1953), pp. 290–91.
7. Keith Garebian, 'Strategy and Theme in the Art of R. K. Narayan', *Ariel* 5, no. 4, (1974): 71.
8. R. K. Narayan, *My Days* (New Delhi: Penguin India, 2006), p. 129.
9. Raja Rao, *Kanthapura* (Delhi: Oxford University Press, 1938), p. v.
10. R. K. Narayan, *A Writer's Nightmare* (New Delhi: Penguin India, 2000), p. 26.

1, Vellala Street

1. A fictional village in South America that serves as the setting for most of Gabriel Garcia Marquez's fiction, like Faulkner's Yoknapatawpha country.
2. A small town in Magdalena province of Colombia, where Garcia Marquez grew up in his maternal grandparents' home, and which, by the author's own admission, contributed to the making of Macondo.
3. *R. K. Narayan: The Early Years, 1906–1945*, p. 6.
4. *My Days*, p. 28.
5. *R. K. Narayan: The Early Years, 1906–1945*, p. 24.
6. *My Days*, p. 2.
7. Ibid., p. 28.
8. Gabriel Garcia Marquez, *Living to Tell the Tale.* (New York: Vintage International, 2004).

School Days in Madras and Mysore

1. R. K. Narayan. *Swami and Friends* (Chicago: University of Chicago Press, 1994), p. 4.
2. *My Days*, p. 34. 3.
3. Ibid., p. 59.
4. Ibid., p. 60.
5. *R. K. Narayan: The Early Years, 1906–1945*, p. 72. 6.
6. Ibid., p. 74.

Making of the Author's Mind

1. *My Days*, p. 65.
2. Ibid., p. 65.
3. Ibid., p. 66.
4. *A Writer's Nightmare*, p. 67.
5. Ibid., p. 7.
6. Ibid., p. 8.
7. R.K. Narayan, 'Remembering Professor J.C. Rollo', *The Literary Criterion* 2 (1978): 5–6.

Becoming a Writer: A Leap of Faith

1. *My Days*, p. 68.
2. Ibid., p. 69.
3. Ibid., p. 73.
4. Ibid., p. 83.
5. Ibid., p. 34.
6. *R. K. Narayan: The Early Years, 1906–1945*, p. 98.

Rajam & the Mysore City Reporter

1. *My Days*, p. 101.
2. Ibid., p. 117.
3. Ibid., p. 118.
4. *R. K. Narayan: The Early Years, 1906–1945*, pp. 126–7.
5. *My Days*, p. 152.
6. Ibid., p. 150.
7. R. K. Narayan, *The English Teacher* (Chennai: Indian Thought Publications, 2007), p. 89.

'Novel Taken. Graham Greene Responsible'

1. *My Days*, p. 127.
2. *R. K. Narayan: The Early Years, 1906–1945*, p. 151.
3. *My Days*, p. 128.
4. *R. K. Narayan: The Early Years, 1906–1945*, p. 154.
5. *My Days*, p. 128.
6. It was somewhat a coincidence. When Narayan was 15, one day a Nelson representative had come from the UK to meet his father to fix a deal about supplying books to the school library. After the meeting was over, Narayan had approached the man sheepishly asking if they would publish his novel the day he managed to write one. 'Undoubtedly,' said the man.
7. Olivia Manning, 'Fiction', *The Spectator*, December 3, 1948.

8. *My Days*, p. 132.
9. Susan Ram and N. Ram, 'R. K. Narayan' *The Guardian*, May 14, 2001, https://www.theguardian.com/news/2001/may/14/guardianobituaries.books

Malgudi: An Imaginary Homeland

1. R. K. Narayan. Author's Introduction to *Malgudi Days* (New York: Penguin Books, 2006), pp. 1–3.
2. *My Days*, p. 87.
3. In actuality, it is a North Indian river which originates from the Nandakot hills in Uttarakhand. The town of Ayodhya, considered holy by the Hindus, is situated on its bank in Uttar Pradesh. In *The Ramayana*, Rama, Sita and Lakshmana cross the river on a boat on their way to *vanavas*.
4. *R. K. Narayan: The Early Years, 1906–1945*, p. 6.
5. Ibid., p. 106.
6. Archana Nathan, 'Where is RK Narayan's Malgudi? It depends on whom you are asking', *Scroll.in*, June 5, 2017, https://scroll.in/reel/838673/where-is-rk-narayans-malgudi-itdepends-on-whom-you-are-asking
7. John Thieme, *R. K. Narayan (Contemporary World Writers)* (New Delhi: Viva Books, 2010), p. 150.
8. John Thieme, 'The Cultural Geography of Malgudi', *The Journal of Commonwealth Literature* 42, no. 2 (2007): 113–126.
9. Jhumpa Lahiri, Introduction to *Malgudi Days* by R. K. Narayan (New York: Penguin Books, 2006), p. 11.
10. Charles Nicholl, 'Re-reading R. K. Narayan'. *The Guardian*, May 14, 2011, https://www.theguardian.com/books/2011/may/14/rk-narayan-malgudi- south-india

Novelizing India

1. *My Days*, p. 132.
2. *A History of Indian English Literature*, p. 169.
3. *R.K. Narayan (Contemporary World Writers)*, p. 78.
4. *A History of Indian Literature in English*, p. 171.
5. *R.K. Narayan (Contemporary World Writers)*, p. 150.
6. *My Days*, p. 21.
7. Ibid., p. 122.
8. Ibid., pp. 209–10.
9. *A Writer's Nightmare*, p. 8.

A Myriad-minded Man

1. *My Days*, p. 197.
2. K. Natwar Singh, 'Our Man in Malgudi', *Frontline*, December 13, 1997, https://frontline.thehindu.com/other/article30160561.ece.
3. Ibid.
4. Ibid.
5. R.K. Narayan, 'Cruelty to Children,' *A Story-Teller's World* (New Delhi: Penguin India, 1989), pp. 72–3.
6. N. Ram, 'I am giving you a lot of trouble', *Rediff.com*, May 15, 2001 https://www.rediff.com/news/2001/may/15spec.htm.
7. Ibid.
8. Zac O'Yeah, 'Meeting Mr Narayan', *The Hindu*, March 12, 2006, http:// www.hindu.com/lr/2006/12/03/stories/2006120300140300.htm.

SELECT BIBLIOGRAPHY

Primary Sources:

Narayan, R. K. *My Days*, Chennai: Indian Thought Publications, 2006.

Ram, Susan and N. Ram, *R K Narayan The Early Years: 1906–1945*. Viking, 1996.

Secondary Sources:

Beatina, Mary. *Narayan: A Study in Transcendence*. New York: Peter Lang, 1994.

Bharucha, Nilufer. 'Colonial Enclosures and Autonomous Spaces: Narayan's Malgudi,' *South Asian Review* 23, no. 1 (2002): 129–153.

Contemporary Collections, Howard Gottlieb Archival Research Centre, Mugar Memorial Library, Boston University, Holding no.: 737, Accessed January 18, 2023, https://www.bu.edu/library/files/2022/05/Gotlieb_Contemporary_Collection_Names.pdf

Garebian, Keith. 'Strategy and Theme in the Art of R K Narayan,' *Ariel* 5, no. 4 (1974): 70–81.

Greene, Graham. Introduction to *The Bachelor of Arts*, by R.K. Narayan London: T. Nelson & Sons, 1937.

Greene, Graham. Introduction to *The Financial Expert*, by R. K. Narayan, London: Methuen, 1952.

Holmstorm, Lakshmi. *The Novels of R K Narayan*. Calcutta: Writers Workshop, 1973.

Iyengar, K R Srinivasa. *Indian Writing in English*. Bombay: Asia Publishing House, 1973.

Mukherjee, Meenakshi. *The Twice Born Fiction: Themes and Techniques of the Indian Novel in English*. New Delhi and London: Heinemann, 1971.

Oliver, Myrna. 'R.K. Narayan; Wry Novelist Brought India to the World', *LA Times*, May 14, 2001, https:// www.latimes.com/archives/la-xpm-2001-may-14-me-63349-story.html

Ramanan, Mohan. *R K Narayan: An Introduction (Contemporary Indian Writers in English)*. Bengaluru: Foundation Books, 2013.

Rao, Ranga. *R K Narayan*. New Delhi: Sahitya Akademi, 2004.

Rao, Raja. *Kanthapura*. New Delhi: Orient Paperbacks, 1992.

Srinath, C. N., eds. *R K Narayan: An Anthology of Recent Criticism*. New Delhi: Pencraft, 2000.

Thieme, John. *R K Narayan (Contemporary World Writers)*. New Delhi: Viva Books, 2010.

Walsh, William. *R K Narayan: A Critical Appreciation*. London: Heinemann, 1982.

LIST OF RK NARAYAN'S WORKS

Fiction

1935 Swami and Friends
1937 The Bachelor of Arts
1938 The Dark Room
1945 The English Teacher
1949 Mr. Sampath—The Printer of Malgudi
1952 The Financial Expert
1955 Waiting for the Mahatma
1958 The Guide
1961 The Man-Eater of Malgudi
1967 The Vendor of Sweets
1976 The Painter of Signs
1983 A Tiger for Malgudi
1986 Talkative Man
1990 The World of Nagaraj
1993 Grandmother's Tale

Non-Fiction

1939 Mysore, Mysore
1960 Next Sunday

1964 My Dateless Diary
1974 Reluctant Guru
1974 My Days
1980 The Emerald Route
1988 A Writer's Nightmare
1989 A Story-Teller's World

Collections of short stories

1943 Malgudi Days (19 Stories)
1943 Dodu and Other Stories (17)
1945 Cyclone and Other Stories (18)
1947 An Astrologer's Day and Other Stories (30/6 of them new)
1956 Lawley Road (33/17 new)
1970 A Horse and Two Goats (5)
1982 Malgudi Days (32/8 new)
1985 Under the Banyan Tree (28)
1993 Salt and Sawdust: Stories and Table Talk

Mythology

1965 Gods, Demons and Others
1972 The Ramayana
1978 The Mahabharata
1995 The Indian Epics Retold

ACKNOWLEDGEMENTS

My introduction to RK Narayan happened rather late in life, while I was in my final year in college. Many from my generation knew him from their childhood days, either through his books or through the wonderful Doordarshan TV series called *Malgudi Days* based on his short stories, in the late 1980s and early '90s. I was familiar with neither. Then one day, a man with salt-and-pepper hair entered the Shakespeare Gallery, where the final year classes for English Honours students were held in my college, with a copy of *The Guide* in hand. It was the beginning of a love affair that stood the test of time, though sadly, Raju's (the mercurial hero of the novel) eventually didn't.

Hence, the person who should be acknowledged at the outset is Professor Satyaki Pal, who introduced me to Narayan's literary world, and by his brilliant teaching of the novel, had perhaps unknowingly sown the seeds of this book, many a summer ago, in a college classroom. I, and I believe whoever attended his lectures on *The Guide* over the years, can still hear his words ringing in our ears: 'Raju is the guide, not only to the travellers to Malgudi, but also to the villagers of Mangal. And Raju is the guide to Rosie as well…' His hair has turned all silky white, and he is now more of a friend, philosopher and guide to me. He took keen interest in me writing this book—from the germination of the idea to the execution, lent me books from his personal collection and guided me in moments of doubts and confusions. Satyaki *da* continues to be the biggest inspiration behind this book, and behind any worthwhile pursuit I undertake in life.

I should be erring in judgement if I don't express my gratitude to Dr Nirmal Kanti Bhattacharjee too, right at the beginning. By instructing me to take this task up, he has shown a faith in me that not many have. Coming from someone who commands the highest respect from the who's who of the literary world, it gave me the self-belief and impetus required by anybody working on his first book. I also take this opportunity to thank my ex-pupil, Arkaprabha Biswas, and now my editor, and all the other members at Niyogi Books, my publisher, for making this monograph happen.

Another person who richly deserves to be acknowledged is Sri Tarun Shaw—Tarun *da* to thousands of book lovers in Calcutta—who moved earth and heaven to find any book, magazine or article, however elusive they might be, that I demanded for my research. He also shared with me many pearls of wisdom about the publishing world, that definitely helped me as a first-time author.

One doesn't really thank one's family, but the least I can do is to express my deepest gratitude to my parents and my wife, for everything. Particularly for each and every occasion when they chose not to bother me with worldly concerns believing I might be busy at work, though more often than not, I was not. I appreciate their sound judgement! However cliched it may sound, this book would not have been possible without them or without the constant support of Mimi, my sister, who spent many an afternoon with me talking about literature and refining my tastes.

Many years ago, a precious friend had presented me a beautiful pen and called me her favourite writer. Till then, I had hardly written anything other than newspaper articles. I am not sure of the favourite part, but today I can at least call myself a writer. Last but not the least, I thank God for making that happen.